The Mysterious Sign to the House of David

The Mysterious Sign to the House of David

Douglas Daudelin

Quotations from the Scriptures are generally taken from the King James Version (but with Old English conversions: ye changed to you, etc.), though in some cases have been supplied by the author, primarily in a small number of cases where a more literal translation of a Hebrew word or words was significant, and in all cases are not copyrighted. Otherwise:

Copyright © 2001 by Douglas Daudelin. All rights reserved.

Published by Word Of Grace And Truth, P.O. Box 325, Allamuchy, NJ 07820-0325

Printed in Korea

Portions of this book may be copied and distributed to facilitate group discussion if the copies are not sold. Portions of it, not exceeding 25% of the total, may be quoted in other writings (whether or not for profit) if the meanings in this book of the portions quoted are not misrepresented and copyright acknowledgement is given. This book may be reproduced and distributed in its entirety if it is not done for profit. Such reproductions must include the entire text and copyright acknowledgement. All other rights reserved. No part of this book may be reproduced for other uses without prior written permission from the author.

ISBN 1-58930-038-6
Library of Congress Control Number: 2001118699

Contents

Chapter 1. A Mysterious Sign 7

Chapter 2. The Context Of The Sign 11

Chapter 3. One Interpretation Of The Sign 37

Chapter 4. A Different Interpretation Of The Sign ... 45

Chapter 5. The Name Of This Son 61

Chapter 6. Could God Become A Man? 73

Chapter 7. Who Can See A Virgin With Child? 83

Chapter 8. Curds And Honey 91

Chapter 9. A Man's House 97

Chapter 10. What Shall We Say Then? 115

Chapter One

A Mysterious Sign

During the time Ahaz was king of Judah, two kings began to attack him, and he was afraid. The prophet Isaiah was sent to Ahaz to tell him that God would deliver Judah from those two kings. After that prophecy, a mysterious sign was promised to the house of David, which is recorded in Isaiah 7:14. The promise was made in Hebrew, and is shown on the front cover of this book. A literal, English translation of that promise is:

"Therefore, shall give the Lord himself to you a sign; behold, ha'almah with child, and will bear a son and will call his name Immanu'el ['With Us God']." Isaiah 7:14

There is disagreement over the meaning of the Hebrew word "ha'almah [העלמה]" in the passage above. Therefore, it is simply transliterated in the above translation. The sign is mysterious because common explanations of this sign, and its fulfillment, do not appear to make sense.

Some say that the purpose of the promised sign was to show that God would deliver Judah from the two kings, and was fulfilled when a young, married woman, pregnant at the time the prophet spoke, gave birth to a son and named him Immanuel. But there are some problems with this interpretation. Why should a woman giving birth to a son and naming him Immanuel, confirm to God's people that he would deliver them from those kings? Is that so unusual? And if that sign was fulfilled in those days, why isn't its fulfillment indicated in the Hebrew Scriptures (the Tanach) – as is the fulfillment of all other signs that the Lord gave for the purpose of showing he would accomplish something he had spoken?

It is said in the New Testament that the sign promised in Isaiah 7:14 was fulfilled when Mary, who is said to have been a virgin, was pregnant with Jesus. But this assertion raises more questions. How could a sign occurring about 700 years later confirm to the house of David that God would indeed deliver them from those kings? Does it make any sense at all to talk about Jesus in Isaiah 7:14? And what kind of sign is that? Can it be proved that Mary was a virgin?

This is a mysterious sign. This book carefully examines the passage with its context and problems. It is written to be understandable to those not familiar with the Hebrew Scriptures, yet at the same time challenging to those who have studied long. It does not shrink back from asking difficult questions. As a result, it addresses many issues of contemporary interest to both Jewish and Gentile people alike.

Can a prophecy in the Hebrew Scriptures of a future event be written in the past tense? If the Messiah is not fathered by one of David's descendants, how could he be of the seed of David? According to the Hebrew Scriptures, is it possible for God to become a man? Do they ever indicate that the Messiah would offer himself as a sacrifice for the sins of others? Is it possible for the Messiah, who is from the tribe of Judah, to be a priest? The Scriptures say that all the seed of Israel will be saved with an everlasting salvation. Does that mean all Jewish people will be saved? Can Gentiles be saved? Most Jewish people believe the Messiah has not yet come. If Jesus is indeed the Jewish Messiah, then most Jewish people today would be rejecting their own Messiah. Do the Hebrew Scriptures speak of a time when most Jewish people would reject their own Messiah? These are some of the issues faced by this book.

In order that those who are not familiar with the Hebrew Scriptures may follow the issues and problems, necessary background is simply, yet carefully, explained as needed. What is a sign? What is the house of David? What is a prophet? Why should we believe what Isaiah wrote? When different English translations of the same passage from the Hebrew Scriptures disagree with one another, how is it possible for a person to understand the passage? As these and other questions are addressed, the Hebrew Scriptures themselves are the source from which the answers are sought.

Chapter Two

The Context Of The Sign

We know that the context of a sentence is often important in coming to a right understanding of its meaning. A sentence may seem to mean something out of its context which, when placed in its proper context, would not make sense. This is also true of things written in the Hebrew Scriptures. Furthermore, a sentence understood to mean something that appears to make sense in its immediate context, yet appears to contradict other statements in the broader context of the Hebrew Scriptures, may not be understood so well after all. We would do well then, in trying to obtain a better understanding of this mysterious sign with such widely differing interpretations, to carefully examine the context.

The Setting

The setting of the prophecies spoken in Isaiah 7 is a simple one. Two kings had joined together to fight against Judah, and all Judah was afraid. This occurred during the time Ahaz was the king of Judah. The beginning of the chapter describes this setting, "And it came to pass in the days of Ahaz ... king of Judah, that Rezin the king of Syria, and Pekah the ... king of Israel, went up toward Jerusalem to war against it ... And it was told the house of David ... And his heart was moved, and the heart of his people, as the trees of the wood are moved with the wind." (Isaiah 7:1-2).

The LORD told the prophet Isaiah to go with his son, Shearjashub (meaning: a remnant will return), to meet Ahaz and speak to him what the Lord commanded him to say. This is reported in Isaiah 7:3-4: "Then said the LORD to Isaiah, 'Go forth now to meet Ahaz, you, and Shearjashub your son ... And say to him ...'". If others besides these three were present when Isaiah spoke the prophecies recorded in Isaiah 7, it was not significant to name them.

Two Prophecies And A Command

The Lord told Ahaz, through the prophet Isaiah, that the two kings would not succeed to conquer Judah: "do not fear, and do not let your heart be timid, because of the two [kings who are] ... saying, 'Let us go up against Judah ... and break her for ourselves, and set a king in her midst' ... Thus saith the Lord GOD, 'It shall not stand, neither shall it come to pass.'" (Isaiah 7:4-7). This prophecy was stated as a fact – there were no conditions on its fulfillment. The Lord told Ahaz that (in his kindness and mercy toward him and all of Judah) he would deliver them from their current trial. There was present another testimony of God's goodness to Judah, the meaning of Isaiah's son's name (who was there with his father): "a remnant will return." A second prophecy appears in verse 8 ("within threescore and five years shall Ephraim be broken, that it be not a people"), but that is not important to understanding the sign given later. Notice that in the above passage, Ahaz was also commanded not to be fearful in this trial.

A Warning

The Lord then warned Ahaz, "If you will not believe [תאמינו], surely you shall not be established [תאמנו]." (Isaiah 7:9). What does that mean? There is a condition and a consequence: If you will not believe in the Lord your God, who has just told you that he will deliver you from the two kings attacking Judah, then you shall not be established. To "be established" here means to "be made to stand faithfully".[1] This warning corresponds with God's previous command to Ahaz not to fear. If Ahaz is ruled over by fear, because he does not believe in the God who said he would deliver him from this trial, then he will not stand faithfully before God.

A very similar situation is recorded in 2 Chronicles 20, and sheds light on this one. A "great multitude" came against Judah and Jehoshaphat the king of Judah to battle against them, "And Jehoshaphat feared, and set himself to seek the LORD, and proclaimed a fast throughout all Judah." (2 Chronicles 20:2-3). Then a prophet, Jahaziel, told them that

---

[1]Those who know Hebrew, or consult an Analytical Hebrew Lexicon, will recognize that the two words from the Hebrew Scriptures translated "believe" and "be established" above, are different inflections of the same Hebrew verb – אמן (inflected in the Hiphil future and Niphal future forms, respectively).

the Lord commanded them not to fear, because he would deliver them from those armies. "And they rose early in the morning, and went forth into the wilderness of Tekoa [to battle against them]: and as they went forth, Jehoshaphat stood and said, 'Hear me, O Judah, and you inhabitants of Jerusalem; Believe [האמינו] in the LORD your God, so shall you be established [ותאמנו]; believe his prophets, so shall you prosper.'" (2 Chronicles 20:20).[2] Jehoshaphat then appointed singers to praise and thank God as they went to the battle. And when they arrived, "they looked unto the multitude and behold, they were dead bodies fallen to the earth" (2 Chronicles 20:24).

· Although the prophet spoke the warning here in Isaiah 7:9 to Ahaz (and similar verb inflections in this passage are singular in what is spoken to him), the "you" implicit in the two inflections of the Hebrew verb "אמן" is plural – meaning "you and your people". For in the doing, it will be all of Judah who, under Ahaz' leadership, are either faithful or unfaithful.

However, it was Ahaz who was warned because a king who believes may also stir up a nation to act faithfully (as Jehoshaphat did in the passage above). But when has either Judah or Israel acted faithfully under an unfaithful king? If the king commands, "Retreat!", who will not retreat?

---

[2]The two words "believe" and "be established" are the Hiphil imperative and Niphal future inflections of the same Hebrew verb "אמן" found in Isaiah 7:9.

But Also, A Provision!

Immediately following the sober warning to Ahaz in verse 9, "the LORD spoke again to Ahaz, saying, 'Ask for yourself a sign from the LORD your God; ask it either in the depth, or in the height above.'" (Isaiah 7:10-11). The Lord commanded Ahaz to ask for a sign "for yourself" (Ahaz).

What Is A Sign?

What is a "sign" in the Hebrew Scriptures? The Hebrew word for "sign" (אות) occurs seventy-seven times in the Scriptures. Eighteen of those times it occurs together with its close cousin, a "wonder" (מופת or מפת) – as in, "signs and wonders". The Hebrew word for "wonder" occurs thirty-five times. In the Scriptures, a sign or wonder is an act, event, or physical display, which is something to be wondered at because it is unusual, unexpected, improbable, or impossible.

The word "sign" first appears in the Scriptures in the first chapter of the first book: "And God said, Let there be lights in the firmament of the heaven to divide the day from the night; and let them be for **signs**, and for seasons, and for days, and years: And let them be for lights" (Genesis 1:14-15). We are taught there that God created the sun, moon, and stars not only for their apparent function – to give light, and to mark days and times – but also to be used by God to give signs in the heavens. For example, the sign which the Lord gave Hezekiah to show that he would accomplish what he had spoken to him, was to bring the **sun** *back* ten degrees on the sundial from what it had previously gone down (Isaiah

38:7-8). Some other signs given by the lights in the heavens are described in Exodus 10:1,21-22 and Joel 3:3-4(2:30-31).[3] [Note: You may find the referenced passage at either Joel 3:3-4 or Joel 2:30-31, depending on your Bible's verse numbering scheme. When a referenced passage has different verse numbers, the common Jewish numbering is shown first in this book.]

What Is The Purpose Of A Sign?

The purpose of a sign or wonder in the Scriptures is to promote belief in, or knowledge of, something. For example, when the Lord sent Moses to bring the sons of Israel out of Egypt, "Moses answered and said, 'But, behold, they will not believe me and will not listen to my voice, for they will say, "The LORD has not appeared to you."'" (Exodus 4:1). The Lord then gave Moses signs to do (e.g., turning his staff into a serpent), "so they **may** believe that the LORD ... has appeared to you" (Exodus 4:5), and would therefore listen to Moses. We are later told that in that case it had the intended result, "and he did the signs before the people. And the people believed" (Exodus 4:30-31). Signs do not always result in belief, for in Numbers 14:11, "the LORD said to Moses, 'How long will this people provoke me? and how long will it be

---

[3] "And the LORD said unto Moses, 'Go in unto Pharaoh: for I have hardened his heart, and the heart of his servants, that **I might show these my signs** before him' ... And the LORD said unto Moses, 'Stretch out your hand toward heaven, that there may be darkness over the land of Egypt, even darkness which may be felt.' And Moses stretched forth his hand toward heaven; and there was a thick darkness in all the land of Egypt three days" (Exodus 10:1,21-22).

"And **I will show wonders** in the heavens and in the earth, blood, and fire, and pillars of smoke. The sun shall be turned into darkness, and the moon into blood, before the great and the terrible day of the LORD come." (Joel 3:3-4(2:30-31)).

until they believe me, for all the signs which I have showed among them?'"

Why Ask For A Sign?

What was the purpose of this command that Ahaz should ask for a sign 'for himself'? It was to help Ahaz believe in the God who will accomplish what he had just spoken, who will deliver Judah from the two kings. A sign, as used in this context, is something that the Lord causes to happen in order to help those seeing the sign believe that he will do what he has spoken.

The Lord offered to give Ahaz any sign he wants – *whatever* he thinks will help him to believe that God will do what he said he would do. Moreover, the Lord encouraged Ahaz to ask for a *tremendous* sign, "ask it either in the depth, or in the height above", or as a similar, modern expression goes, "the sky's the limit." The Lord does not make an idle offer here. The one who created both the heights above and the depths beneath – his arm is not cut short to do whatever he desires in them. As it is written, "Ah Lord GOD! behold, you have made the heaven and the earth by your great power and stretched out arm, and there is nothing too hard for you" (Jeremiah 32:17).

This offer to Ahaz was indeed extraordinary. There is no other offer like this recorded in all the Scriptures.

Why Wouldn't Ahaz Believe What God Said?

It is helpful to consider, that although we are told here the LORD (יהוה) spoke these words to Ahaz, they were spoken to the king through a *man* – Isaiah. Ahaz saw Isaiah speaking to him. But the prophet Isaiah spoke the words that the Lord put in his mouth – the words he spoke to Ahaz were God's words, not his own. Therefore it was that, "**the LORD spoke** again to Ahaz …" (verse 10). It was also earlier stated by Isaiah that he spoke in the name of the Lord when he said, "Thus saith the Lord GOD, …" (Isaiah 7:7).

This is not something unique to Isaiah's utterance, but all of the prophets, when they spoke in the name of the Lord, spoke God's words; as it is written, "And **the LORD** spoke by his servants **the prophets**" (2 Kings 21:10). That is why Jehoshaphat, after saying, "Believe in the LORD your God, so shall you be established", said, "believe his prophets, so shall you prosper." (2 Chronicles 20:20). For through his prophets (*his* prophets, that is, not false prophets), God has made known who he is and what his will is. Because of this, David said, "The Spirit of the LORD spoke by me, and his word was in my tongue." (2 Samuel 23:2). In the same way, the words that Isaiah wrote to us in his book are God's words, not Isaiah's. In the second verse of the book of Isaiah it is written, "Hear, O heavens, and give ear, O earth: for the LORD has spoken" (Isaiah 1:2). In the book of Jeremiah, the Lord gave an extended account of how the words he spoke through Jeremiah came to be written, "And … this word came unto Jeremiah from the LORD, saying, 'Take a roll of a book, and write therein all the words that I have spoken unto you … from the days of Josiah, even unto this day.' … Then Jeremiah called Baruch the son of Neriah: and Baruch wrote from the mouth of Jeremiah all the words of the LORD, which he had spoken unto him, upon a roll of a book. ... And they asked Baruch, saying, 'Tell us now, How did you write all these words at his mouth?' Then Baruch answered them, 'He pronounced all these words unto me with his mouth, and I wrote them with ink in the book.'" (Jeremiah 36:1-2,4,17-18).

Some may ask, "Why has God usually spoken through prophets, rather than directly to all people?" While that question is beyond the scope of this book, it is interesting to note that when God did speak to all the people of Israel from the heavens, they begged Moses, "let not God speak with us, lest we die." (Exodus 20:16(19)), "You go near, and hear all that the LORD our God shall say: and you speak to us all that the LORD our God shall speak to you; and we will hear it, and do it." (Deuteronomy 5:24(27)).

A *Command* To Ask For A Sign?

It is very unusual for the Lord to command someone to ask for a sign to help him believe. In fact, there is no other place in the Scriptures where God commanded someone to ask for a sign. In other places, people have asked the Lord to give them a sign to help them believe, or the Lord, unasked, said he would give a sign. It is a most gracious command, given the warning that has just been spoken to Ahaz about the importance of him believing. Note that it is a command, not an invitation such as, "If you like, ask …".

Why does the Lord do this? It is because "the LORD looks on the heart" (1 Samuel 16:7), and sees that Ahaz does not believe. He knows the evil Ahaz will do, and the trouble he will bring on himself and all Judah, if he continues in his unbelief. And the Lord, desiring to do good to Ahaz and to Judah, gives him this gracious command. Such is the character of God, who says, "I have spread out my hands all the day to a rebellious people. ... A people that provoke me to anger continually to my face; ... Which say, 'Stand by yourself, come not near to me; for I am holier than you.'" (Isaiah 65:2-3,5). It is this aspect of God's character that Jonah complained about, in anger that God had mercy on Nineveh, "But it displeased Jonah exceedingly, and he was very angry. ... and said, '... **Therefore** I fled before to Tarshish: for I knew that you are a gracious God, and merciful, slow to anger, and of great kindness'" (Jonah 4:1-2).

The Refusal

In the next verse, we are told Ahaz' response, "But Ahaz said, 'I will not ask, neither will I test the LORD.'" (Isaiah 7:12). Ahaz refused God's command to him, even though it was for his good. However, regardless of whether it was for his good or harm, it was still a command from God. Further, he gave a "righteous" reason for doing so, as if to say, 'Far be it from the righteous Ahaz to do such an evil thing as to test the Lord by asking for a sign!' By his answer, he also implies that he does not need to ask a sign in order to believe God will do what he has spoken through the mouth of his prophet. Did Ahaz *indeed* refuse the evil thing *God* had commanded him to do, and instead choose that which is good? Is it not *rather* that he refused the good (to obey God's gracious command), and chose in its place the evil (to rebel against God's command and remain in his unbelief)? The cause of his rebellion appears to be a proud heart – being unwilling to accept that he needs a sign to believe what God has said through Isaiah – yet he justifies himself by saying he is doing good.

Saying Of Evil: This Is Good

Ahaz' action is an example of what God earlier charged against the "inhabitants of Jerusalem, and men of Judah", "that call evil good, and good evil" (Isaiah 5:3,20). The people say of that which is evil – this is good. And they say of that which is good – that is evil. It is not **just** a matter of **doing** that which is evil, for Ahaz did not say only, "I will not ask". It is a matter of choosing to do the evil, for the stated reason that it is in fact the good and righteous thing, and that to rather do the good, would in fact be evil. Ahaz refused God's command in order to do that which he said was more righteous than God's command.

Determined Unbelief

In effect, Ahaz is determined to continue in his unbelief despite God's gracious command. In the midst of Ahaz' trial, God spoke to him. Unasked, he sent a prophet to him, and told him he would deliver Judah from the two kings. The name of the prophet's son (Shearjashub – a remnant will return) was a reminder to Ahaz of God's eternal good will toward Judah. He was warned that he must not fear nor be timid, but believe in the God who said he would deliver him, and take courage, so that he might stand faithfully before God. But, he was also graciously commanded to ask for a sign, in order that he might believe. Make it deep in the depths; make it high in the heavens! Ask! and the Lord GOD of Israel will do it! Ahaz is told to pick *anything he wants* for a sign, *whatever* he thinks would help him believe. Ahaz does not believe God. But he is not willing to obey the command to ask a sign in order that he might believe. Therefore, he is unwilling to believe.

What More Could Have Been Done?

What more could have been done with Ahaz that the Lord did not do? It is even as the Lord spoke only two chapters earlier of all Judah, "judge, I ask you, between me and my vineyard. What could have been done more to my vineyard that I have not done in it?" (Isaiah 5:3-4). Because Ahaz refused God's command, it is clear from the Hebrew Scriptures that Ahaz did **not** believe, and did not stand faithfully before God during this trial. For example, "And in the time of his distress did he trespass yet more against the LORD: this is that king Ahaz. For he sacrificed unto the gods of Damascus, which smote him: and he said, 'Because the gods of the kings of Syria help them, therefore will I sacrifice to them, that they may help me.'" (2 Chronicles 28:22-23). And, as if that were too little, "Ahaz gathered together the vessels of the house of God, and cut in pieces the vessels of the house of God, and shut up the doors of the house of the LORD" (2 Chronicles 28:24)! Compare Ahaz' actions with the believing king Jehoshaphat's actions described earlier. Because of Ahaz' wickedness, following from his unbelief, there were penalties for him personally, as well as for all Judah. Nevertheless, the two kings did not succeed in conquering Judah, even as the Lord had spoken to him by the prophet

Isaiah. Though Ahaz (and Judah with him) was unfaithful, God was faithful.

The Consequence

The Lord spoke to Ahaz at the end of this chapter to tell him of a subsequent, severe trial he will bring upon him and his people after the two kings depart (see verse 17 and following). This third prophecy was of a trial so severe, that it was said there of those days that they will be "days that have not come, from the day that Ephraim departed from Judah; even the king of Assyria." (Isaiah 7:17). [Note: This king is different from the king of Syria who is part of their present trial.] As a result of that subsequent trial, this is how King Hezekiah (the son of Ahaz who reigned after Ahaz), described the state of Judah and Jerusalem in the first month of his reign, "Wherefore the wrath of the LORD was upon Judah and Jerusalem, and he has delivered them to trouble, to astonishment, and to hissing, as you see with your eyes. For, lo, our fathers have fallen by the sword, and our sons and our daughters and our wives are in captivity for this." (2 Chronicles 29:8-9).

The Last Time

This prophecy in Isaiah 7 of a subsequent trial the Lord will bring upon Ahaz, is the last time he was spoken to in the book of Isaiah, and the Lord did not use his name to address him. In fact, Ahaz' name is found only two more times in the entire book of Isaiah. The next place his name is found is seven chapters later, in Isaiah 14:28 when it says, significantly, "In the year that king Ahaz **died** …". The final place his name is mentioned is when the Lord spoke of a tremendous sign he was going to give Hezekiah (a righteous king) in Isaiah 38:7-8 – to **bring back** the sun ten degrees, from what it had "gone down in the sun dial of Ahaz". It is interesting to consider the symbolism in that reference, but this is not the place to write about it.

Comparing The Circumstances Of The Two Signs

However, it is worth noting some similarities, and a significant difference, between the circumstances surrounding the sign offered to Ahaz in Isaiah 7:10-11, and the sign offered to his son Hezekiah in Isaiah 38.

The Similarities

Both Ahaz and Hezekiah were under siege, and the Lord prophesied to each of them that he would deliver them from their enemies. The prophecy to Hezekiah is in Isaiah 38:6, "I will deliver you and this city out of the hand of the king of Assyria: and I will defend this city [Jerusalem] " At the time of the prophecy to Hezekiah, he was sick and about to die, and the Lord *also* told him he would recover from his sickness and live fifteen more years. Since Hezekiah reigned twenty-nine years, this prophecy must have been spoken in the fourteenth year of his reign. Therefore, the trouble with the king of Assyria mentioned in Isaiah 38:6, is described in Isaiah 36:1, "in the fourteenth year of king Hezekiah, … Sennacherib king of Assyria came up against all the defenced cities of Judah, and took them."

God spoke the prophecies to each of them through the same man – Isaiah. It is helpful to remember that the Lord did not speak from the heavens to these men, but that Isaiah came and told them, "Thus saith the Lord …", just as the Lord has spoken to us all through Isaiah, in the words written by Isaiah here in the book of Isaiah.

The purpose of the sign to Hezekiah was similar to the purpose of the sign offered to Ahaz – that Hezekiah might know "that the LORD will **do** this thing that **he** has **spoken**" (Isaiah 38:7).

The Difference

But there is a significant difference between the circumstances of Hezekiah's sign, and the sign his father Ahaz was commanded to ask. Hezekiah, knowing that it was important for him to believe what the Lord had spoken to him by way of Isaiah, but also knowing his own unbelief, **asked** for a sign (Isaiah 38:22, as also 2 Kings 20:8-10). Ahaz refused a sign which he, alone of all, was commanded by God to ask, whereas his son did request a sign.

Why the Difference?

Why did Hezekiah behave so differently from his father? Hezekiah was 9 years old when his father began to reign as king of Judah ("Ahaz … reigned sixteen years in Jerusalem" 2 Kings 16:2, "Twenty and five years old was he when he [Hezekiah] began to reign [after Ahaz' reign ended]" 2 Kings 18:2). He learned from observing and living through the trial brought on Judah by the Lord during his father's reign, while knowing why it had come. For when Hezekiah began his reign he said, "For our **fathers** have trespassed, and done that which was evil in the eyes of the LORD our God, and **have forsaken him**, ... **Wherefore** the wrath of the LORD was upon Judah and Jerusalem" (2 Chronicles 29:6,8). Because Hezekiah knew the trial that came upon Judah resulted from their rebellion against the Lord, he and others from Judah who had escaped with him, learned to refuse the evil and choose the good.

Hear Now, O House Of David

Immediately following Ahaz' refusal in Isaiah 7:12, the Lord addressed the house of David: "And he said, 'Hear now, O house of David ...'" (Isaiah 7:13). Some may object, "Where is the house of David? All we know about here is Isaiah, his son, and Ahaz." Nevertheless, that is to whom the Lord spoke. But that is not unusual, for he spoke to Babylon in Isaiah 13:1, Moab in 15:1, Egypt in 19:1, and Tarshish in 23:1. He spoke to all people of the earth in Isaiah 34:1. And the Lord began the book of Isaiah by calling the heavens and earth to hear his complaint against Judah and Jerusalem, saying, "Hear heavens, and give ear earth, for the LORD has spoken: I have grown and brought up sons, but they have rebelled against me." (Isaiah 1:2).

However, the Lord also caused his words to the house of David to be written plainly here in Isaiah 7, for a testimony to the house of David and all who read the Scriptures in every generation. In an English translation of Isaiah 7:13-14, the word "you" appears three or four times, and is plural in the Hebrew text in each place (i.e., "you all"). This agrees with whom the Lord addressed – those in the house of David.

A Complaint

In Isaiah 7:13, the Lord began with a complaint and charge against the house of David. "And he said, 'Hear now, O house of David; Is it a small thing for you to weary men, but will you weary my God also?'" To avoid confusion, note that here and in the rest of this seventh chapter the prophet Isaiah speaks in the first person. Accordingly, he says, "my God", rather than, "me." As he also says, in verse 17, "The LORD", rather than "I." Nevertheless, Isaiah is still speaking God's words – he has not digressed into giving his opinion about these things and what will happen in the future.

This complaint raises two related questions. What is the house of David? And why did Ahaz' self-righteous rebellion provoke God to complain against the house of David? In a word, the house of David does not consist of a physical structure, but consists of those born in David's house, women married to men in the house of David, and their slaves (not hired servants). A more complete answer and explanation of who is in the house of David according to the Hebrew Scriptures will be given later. However, it is necessary to know some promises God had made in 2 Samuel 7 and 1 Chronicles 17 in order to better understand this complaint against it, as well as the mysterious sign which was promised to it immediately after this complaint.

In both 2 Samuel 7 and 1 Chronicles 17, there is an account of what happened when David desired to build a house for the Lord. The Lord answered him saying, "You shall not build me a house to dwell in" (1 Chronicles 17:4), and, "I tell you that the LORD will build you a house." (1 Chronicles 17:10). At that time, God made a number of wonderful and very important promises to Israel, David, and the house of David. Before looking at the specific promises, it is helpful to observe some differences between the two accounts.

By comparing the two accounts, it can be seen that not all of what the Lord spoke to David was completely recorded in either place. This is not unusual in the Scriptures, where God often gives additional details in a passage about an event described in another passage. An example of this is found in the first two chapters of the first book in the Scriptures, where Genesis 2 gives more details about an event also described in Genesis 1 – especially about how God made the first man and woman. In 2 Samuel 7:12-15, a seed of David is spoken of who will proceed out of David's body and build a house for the name of the Lord. 1 Chronicles 28:6 records that the Lord revealed to David that that seed was Solomon. But in 1 Chronicles 17:11-14, a seed of David is spoken of who will build a house for the Lord, and stand in God's house and God's kingdom forever. This is a different seed of David than Solomon – for Solomon died and his reign ended. This refers to the seed of David who is the Messiah. More will be said about these two seeds when describing the promises below.

Israel God's People Forever,
The House Of David Established Forever

In those passages, God made a promise to Israel, "I will ordain a place for my people Israel, and will plant them, and they shall dwell in their place, and shall be moved **no more**; neither shall the sons of wickedness waste them **any more**, as at the beginning" (1 Chronicles 17:9). David, praising and thanking God afterward, said, "For your people Israel you have made your own people **forever**; and you, LORD, have become their God." (1 Chronicles 17:22).

God also promised to establish the house of David and the kingdom of David before God forever, "And your house and your kingdom shall be established forever before you: your throne shall be established forever." (2 Samuel 7:16). David afterward praised and thanked God for these promises, saying, "For you, my God, have told your servant that you will build him a house ... And now, LORD, you are God, and have promised this goodness to your servant: And now it has pleased you to bless the house of your servant, that it may be before you forever: for you have blessed, LORD, and it shall be blessed **forever**." (1 Chronicles 17:25-27).

The Messiah, King Forever

These promises to Israel, David, and the house of David are related to, and are brought to pass by, another promise God made here: that the Lord will raise up one from David's seed after him, and **he** will reign in God's house and in God's kingdom **forever**. "And it shall come to pass, ... that I will raise up your seed after you, who shall be of your sons; and I will establish his kingdom. ... And I will make **him** stand in my house and in my kingdom **forever**: and his throne shall be established forever." (1 Chronicles 17:11,14). This one from David's seed, from the house of David, is the Messiah.

The Mysterious Sign to the House of David

It is confirmed in other places in the Hebrew Scriptures that the Messiah will literally reign forever. One of those places is in a prophecy of the Messiah given through Daniel, "I saw in the night visions, and, behold, one like the son of man came with the clouds of heaven, and came to the Ancient of days, and they brought him near before him. And there was given him dominion, and glory, and a kingdom, that all people, nations, and languages, should serve him: his dominion is an everlasting dominion, which shall not pass away" (Daniel 7:13-14).

Of course, there are many places in the Scriptures that talk of the Messiah. One is in Jeremiah, "Behold, the days come, says the LORD, that I will raise unto David a righteous Branch, and a King shall reign and prosper, and shall execute judgment and justice in the earth. In his days Judah shall be saved, and Israel shall dwell safely: and this is his name whereby he shall be called, 'The LORD [יהוה] Our Righteousness [צדקנו]'" (Jeremiah 23:5-6). It is important to recognize that the **everlasting** blessings to both Israel and the house of David will be fulfilled through the reign of the Messiah.

Solomon's Kingdom Established Forever (If)

Another promise God made at this time was that one who would come out of David's body would build a house for the name of the Lord, and the throne of *this one's* kingdom would be established forever, "I will set up your seed after you, which shall proceed out of your body, and I will establish his kingdom. He shall build a house for my name, and I will establish the throne of his kingdom forever." (2 Samuel 7:12-13). Of course, it was not said here that this one personally would stand in his kingdom forever, but that the "throne of his kingdom", as the throne of David's kingdom, would be established forever.

However, in 1 Chronicles 28:6-7, there are some additional, very important details given about this promise spoken to David. The one spoken of was identified as Solomon, and the promise to establish the throne of Solomon's kingdom was said to be **conditional** upon Solomon's being constant to keep God's commandments, "And he said unto me, 'Solomon your son, he shall build my house and my courts … Moreover I will establish his kingdom forever, **if** he be constant to do my commandments and my judgments, as at this day.'" (1 Chronicles 28:6-7; as also 2 Chronicles 7:17-18 mentions this condition).

After Solomon built the house (the first temple), it was further said that the **house** he built was for the Lord to put his name there **forever**, "Then spake Solomon, '… I have surely built you a house to dwell in, a settled place for you to abide in forever.' … And the LORD said unto him, 'I have heard your prayer and your supplication, that you have made before me: I have hallowed this house, which you have built, **to put my name there forever**; and my eyes and my heart shall be there perpetually.'" (1 Kings 8:12-13, 1 Kings 9:3). However, in the same way, **if** Solomon **or** his sons reigning on the throne of his kingdom after him did **not** continue in God's commandments, Israel would be cut off out of the land, and the house he built would be cast out of God's sight, "But if you [Solomon] shall at all turn from following me, **you or your sons**, and will not keep my commandments and my statutes which I have set before you, but go and serve other gods, and worship them: Then will I cut off Israel out of the land which I have given them; and this house, which I have hallowed for my name, will I cast out of my sight; and Israel shall be a proverb and a byword among all people" (1 Kings 9:6-7; as also 1 Kings 6:12-13 mentions this condition).

It is important to recognize that the blessings to both Israel and the house of David **until** the reign of the Messiah were conditional on whether Solomon, and his sons after him who ruled in Israel, kept God's commandments and statutes. We also see from the history recorded in the Scriptures how Israel prospered under righteous kings, and suffered under unrighteous kings. It is amazing that the righteousness of one man, the leader of the people, determines the well being of the entire nation!

A Summary Of The Promises

The promises made can be categorized as two types. First, unconditional promises to bring forth the Messiah from the house of David, who will reign forever, and in his days will make Israel dwell safely forever and move no more. Second, conditional promises to establish Solomon's kingdom, and the house he would build, and bless Israel in their land without any interruption. Solomon, and his sons reigning on the throne of his kingdom after him, could keep Israel well *until* the coming of the Messiah, if they personally were faithful to keep God's commandments and statutes. However, even if they were not, the Messiah would finally accomplish forever that which Solomon and his sons could not do because of their sinfulness. For the promise eventually to establish David's kingdom over Israel forever was **unconditional:**

"Ought you not to know that the LORD God of Israel gave the kingdom over Israel to David forever, even to him and to his sons by a covenant of salt?" (2 Chronicles 13:5), "for you have blessed, LORD, and it **shall** be blessed **forever**." (1 Chronicles 17:27).

Why This Complaint Against The House Of David?

Now it is clear from verse 13 that the Lord was wearied with the house of David: "Hear now, O house of David; Is it a small thing for you to weary men, but will you weary my God also?" Weariness comes from a wearing down, a pattern of tiresome behavior. And how much more of a pattern when the one who has become wearied is renowned for his strength to be "slow to anger", "longsuffering", and "gracious and merciful"? To weary (לאה) is a verb applied to God only two other times in the Hebrew Scriptures. Ahaz was of Solomon's sons, as were all of the kings of Judah who reigned after Solomon until the time God cast the house Solomon built out of his sight (2 Kings 25:9 – after which none of Solomon's sons have been king). Therefore, Ahaz was of the house of Solomon, and also of the house of David. Ahaz' self-righteous rebellion against God was one more in a long succession of actions by which the house of David wearied God. God desired to bless the house of David and all Israel with it, and he will keep the promise, but its actions continually called for punishment.

First Solomon

Solomon was beloved of God, and God made him king over Israel and blessed him greatly. There was no king like him among many nations. Nevertheless, "it came to pass, when Solomon was old, that his wives turned away his heart after other gods: and his heart was not perfect with the LORD his God, as was the heart of David his father. For Solomon went after Ashtoreth the goddess of the Zidonians, and after Milcom the abomination of the Ammonites. And Solomon did evil in the sight of the LORD ..." (1 Kings 11:4-6). The result, "Wherefore the LORD said unto Solomon, 'Forasmuch as this is done of you, and you have not kept my covenant and my statutes, which I have commanded you, I will surely rend the kingdom from you, and will give it to your servant. Notwithstanding, in your days I will not do it, for David your father's sake: but I will rend it out of the hand of your son. Howbeit, I will not rend away all the kingdom; but will give one tribe to your son for David my servant's sake, and for Jerusalem's sake which I have chosen." (1 Kings 11:11-13). Therefore, Solomon's kingdom was not established. Others were given the rule over the kingdom of Israel, while Solomon's sons were left to rule over Judah for a time.

Then His Sons

Moreover, neither were Solomon's sons careful to keep God's commandments and his statutes. As a result, Judah's state in the first chapter of Isaiah was summarized, "Why should you be stricken any more? you will revolt more and more: the whole head is sick, and the whole heart faint. From the sole of the foot even unto the head there is no soundness in it; but wounds, and bruises, and putrifying sores: they have not been closed, neither bound up, neither mollified with ointment. Your country is desolate, your cities are burned with fire: your land, strangers devour it in your presence, and it is desolate, as overthrown by strangers." (Isaiah 1:5-7). The sad state to which Solomon and his sons have brought all Israel is underscored in the setting of this seventh chapter of Isaiah – the king of Israel has joined with the king of Syria to war against Judah.

Now Ahaz

And now, Ahaz hasn't believed in God's salvation, and therefore he would be unfaithful. According to his word, God would eventually cut off Israel out of the land; and the house Solomon built, which God had hallowed to put his name there forever, he would cast out of his sight. And Solomon's sons would no longer reign, not even over the "one tribe" they had been left.

The Mysterious Sign

After God tells the house of David in Isaiah 7:13 that he is wearied by them, the Lord continues in Isaiah 7:14, "Therefore, shall give the Lord himself to you a sign; behold, ha'almah with child, and will bear a son and will call his name Immanu'el ['With Us God']." Here, finally, this mysterious sign is promised. There is disagreement over the proper translation of the Hebrew word "ha'almah" (העלמה) to represent the meaning of that word about 2700 years ago when the prophet spoke it. Some translate it "young woman," others "maiden," and others "virgin." Whatever its true meaning was, we know it refers to a certain young woman, and that is enough to try to understand the passage in its context. Because of the disagreement, it is simply transliterated here. In that way, the above translation does not bring anything more nor less to the passage than the actual Hebrew word does.

Chapter Three

One Interpretation Of The Sign

Some say this was a sign to confirm that God would deliver Judah from the two kings. They say the sign was that a young, married woman, who was pregnant at the time the prophet spoke, would give birth to a son and name him Immanuel.

Why This Sign?

According to this interpretation, this sign was a "replacement sign" for the one that God had commanded Ahaz to ask for himself in verse 11, but Ahaz refused. The reason for giving the sign would be the same as the one in verse 11: so that Ahaz would not fear, but believe in the Lord and in the salvation he promised through the prophet Isaiah, and thereby have courage to stand faithfully in this trial.

But there are some difficulties with this reason for giving the sign. The sign Ahaz was commanded to ask in verse 11 was for himself. But this sign was not given here specifically to Ahaz, but explicitly to the broader house of David: "Hear now, O house of David ... Therefore, shall give the Lord himself to you [plural] a sign". God was angry with Ahaz for refusing the sign, and for that reason lifted up his voice to speak to the house of David who was "wearing him out." It was the house of David that was then promised this unasked-for sign. However, Ahaz *is* a member of the house of David, and also it will be all of Judah who is either faithful or unfaithful during this national trial. Yet still, Ahaz is the one who needs to believe in order that he might lead Judah faithfully. If the king commands that they should build an altar to the gods of Damascus, and that the doors of the house of the Lord should be shut up, but the king's brother does not agree because he believes in the God who speaks through Isaiah and promised to deliver them – what will Judah do? A king may be killed or dethroned ... but while the king is king, they will do what the king has commanded.

Could the reason have been so that *other* members of the house of David might believe, and their belief and confidence would help *Ahaz* to believe and not fear? Could it be that God's mercy and good will toward Ahaz extended even this far in his rebellion? After all, the fathers of the tribes of Israel did intend evil against their brother Joseph when they sold him as a slave, yet God worked it for their good. For Joseph said, "But as for you, you thought evil against me; but God meant it unto good, to bring to pass, as it is this day, to save much people alive." (Genesis 50:20). However, the context gives an impression that God is unwilling to continue to try to help Ahaz believe – who is determined to

One Interpretation Of The Sign

continue in unbelief. After the Lord speaks to Ahaz one last time at the end of this chapter, to tell him of a severe trial he will bring upon him and all Judah because of his rebellion, he does not speak to him ever again in the book of Isaiah. Further, it is clear in the end that Ahaz did **not** believe that God would deliver Judah from those two kings and remained unfaithful.

Who Performs The Sign?

Another problem arising with this interpretation is by *whose action* the sign is brought to pass. The essence of the sign, according to this interpretation, is the name by which the child spoken about in the sign will be called. For a young woman giving birth is not a sign, but commonplace. Yet, the Lord did not speak in this way, "Do this for a sign, name the son who will be born ...". But he spoke in this way, "Therefore, shall **give** the **Lord** *himself* to you a sign ...". This was a sign which the Lord underscored **he** will **give**, and not a command that **someone** should **do** something.

In the Scriptures, there are examples of the Lord commanding someone to do something for a sign. For example, God commanded Ezekiel to do something as a sign for the people, "and I did in the morning [the unusual thing] as I was commanded. ... [and the Lord said to the people] 'Thus Ezekiel is unto you a sign: according to all that he has done shall you do: and when this comes, you shall know that I am the Lord GOD.'" (Ezekiel 24:18,24). Observe that in Ezekiel's case, the purpose of the sign was to help people believe in God **after** the future, prophesied event took place ("when this comes, [after you are made to do in the future according to all that Ezekiel has done, then] you shall know that I am the

The Mysterious Sign to the House of David

Lord GOD."). For in this way it would be confirmed in people's minds that God indeed spoke through Ezekiel and brought their destruction on them – when it happened to them in the same way Ezekiel had (unusually) acted out before them. When it came to pass, they would *then* **know** it was a judgment of God against them because of their rebellion against God, and not just some 'random disaster' they had suffered at the hands of men. The sign Ezekiel did before them was **not** a sign to help them believe that God **would** do what he had said. It was to help them believe that the Lord is God in all the earth, **when** all he said would take place through his prophet did in fact **come to pass**.

Although there were times the Lord commanded someone to do something for a sign, that did not happen in Isaiah 7:14. Rather, the Lord promised in this passage that he himself would give a sign.

Is This A Tremendous Sign?

Still other difficulties continue with this interpretation of the sign. The context of the passage leads us to expect a *tremendous* sign was promised. For the Lord previously told Ahaz to ask for any sign he desired, and encouraged the king to make it a tremendous sign, "ask it either in the depth, or in the height above". Now that God said he would give a sign, wouldn't we expect it to be at least as wonderful as anything Ahaz may have asked? Or will Ahaz have to settle for some *lesser* miracle, now that God chose the sign? Was the Creator of the heavens and the earth afraid to choose something that might be too *hard* for him to perform? Or, was God *unable* to think of a sign as tremendous as Ahaz could think of? A woman naming her son Immanuel is hardly a tremendous sign. After word of the promised sign spread, we would not be surprised if many women named their son Immanuel.

Is This A Sign At All?

If this sign is a replacement sign for the one God commanded Ahaz to ask for himself in verse 11, then its purpose is to help Ahaz believe in the God who said he would deliver Judah from the two kings. A sign in the Scriptures is a thing of wonder, and therefore, can help the unbelieving to believe. But we must wonder why someone then having a son, and giving him the name Isaiah proclaimed would be given to a son, would be a sign at all.

Some say the woman was either Isaiah's or Ahaz' wife. But that conjecture further robs the sign of any possible impact. What do you think? A prophet comes and says he speaks in the name of the Lord, and the Lord will do this or that. Then he says, "So that you may believe in the God whose words I speak, and believe that he will surely do what I have said, my pregnant wife will have a son, and when she does, we will call his name Immanuel." If you had doubted the prophet's words, would you then be persuaded when that prophet names his son Immanuel? But what if you were to name your son Immanuel, would that persuade you in any way to believe the prophet you had previously doubted? Does any of this make sense?

When Was This Sign Fulfilled?

If there had been such a thing as a Jerusalem newspaper at that time, and we could search copies of it for the year following the promised sign, we would not be surprised to read of ten women (a number of whom were not married) who gave birth to sons and named them Immanuel. Nevertheless, the Hebrew Scriptures do not describe such an event. The two Hebrew words composing the name by which the child who is born will be called (אל and עמנו), occur consecutively as either one or two words only two other times in the Hebrew Scriptures. Interestingly, as will be discussed later, both occurrences are in the very next chapter – Isaiah 8:8,10. Yet, the fulfillment of this sign is not indicated in the Hebrew Scriptures. Every other sign that the Lord gave for the purpose of showing he would accomplish something he had spoken, has its fulfillment indicated in the Hebrew Scriptures. This gives the impression that this sign was not fulfilled before the Hebrew Scriptures were completed.

A Summary

This interpretation of the sign may at first appear to fit well. However, a number of significant problems arise when the context and the passage itself are carefully considered, and when compared with other signs in the Hebrew Scriptures. The *reason* for giving such a sign – to help Ahaz believe in the Lord and in the salvation he promised through the prophet Isaiah, and thereby have courage to stand faithfully in this trial – at best was not accomplished, and at worst does not seem to fit the context. Also, we look for a sign that "**the Lord himself**" would give. But if someone gives their son the name Isaiah previously proclaimed someone would, how is it that "the Lord *himself*" has given that sign? We expect a *tremendous* sign, perhaps the greatest ever given, but this is hardly a tremendous sign. In fact, we are left to wonder whether the sign according to this interpretation is a sign or wonder *at all*. It is hard to see how its coming to pass would promote belief that the Lord would do what he had spoken through the prophet. Finally, all other signs recorded in the Scriptures which the Lord gave to show that he would do what he had spoken, also have their fulfillment indicated in those Scriptures. Therefore, we are left with the impression it was unfulfilled when the Hebrew Scriptures were completed.

Some Variations To This Interpretation

There are some minor variations to the previously offered interpretation of this sign, which do not depart from the basic nature of that interpretation, and have all of the same difficulties mentioned above. For example, the ArtScroll Tanach (Stone Edition) and the Jewish Publication Society's "JPS 1917" translate ha'almah's pregnancy as a future event: "will become pregnant" and "shall conceive". Including this variation in the previously offered interpretation – that a certain, young, married woman would also become pregnant – does not significantly add to the nature of the sign. Further, there is an additional problem with this modified interpretation. Since the young woman would first need to conceive before giving birth and naming the son Immanuel, the sign wouldn't be given until at least nine months after the prophet spoke. Those would be nine long months of siege from two kings attacking a fearful and unbelieving Ahaz.

Another variation arises from the ArtScroll Tanach's translation of almah as "maiden". This translation explicitly says the young woman who would become pregnant was unmarried. Including this variation in the previously offered interpretation introduces a further problem: how did the Lord intend for this maiden to become pregnant? For it is a sin for an unmarried woman to lie with a man.

Chapter Four

A Different Interpretation Of The Sign

The New Testament, Matthew 1:22-23 in particular, says that the sign promised in Isaiah 7:14 was fulfilled when Mary became pregnant with a son – Jesus. Also according to the New Testament, Mary was a virgin (Luke 1:34-35; Matthew 1:18-20,25), and Jesus is that promised one of David's seed, born in the house of David, who is the Messiah (Luke 2:1,4-5, John 1:41,45,49-50, Mark 14:61-62, Acts 13:22-23). There are many objections that may be made to this interpretation. However, it must be admitted that this is a sign about which it *could* be said the Lord himself gave it, and a tremendous sign, which was fulfilled after the Hebrew Scriptures were completed.

Why This Sign?

Why would God promise to give a sign in Isaiah 7:14 which concerns his bringing the promised Messiah into the world? There are two separate, though related, issues here – the purpose of the sign itself, and the reason for giving it in verse 14 of the seventh chapter of Isaiah.

The Mysterious Sign to the House of David

The purpose in giving the sign promised in verse 14 was certainly for blessing the house of David, and not for cursing them. The name of the child alone conveys this: "With Us God." But why would there be a blessing given in the context of Ahaz' rebellion against God? And not in the context of his rebellion alone, but where this has also caused God to remind the house of David in the immediately preceding verse 13 that Ahaz' action is one more in a long line of contrary actions by them? For God will bring judgment on individuals and groups who rebel against him. This truth is stated in the first chapter of Isaiah, "And the destruction of the transgressors and of the sinners shall be together, and they that forsake the LORD shall be consumed." (Isaiah 1:28). As it is also written, "Cursed be he that does not perform all the words of this law to do them. And all the people shall say, Amen." (Deuteronomy 27:26). It is because of this truth that there are consequences of this rebellion to Ahaz, Judah, and the house of David, which are promised later in this chapter, "The LORD shall bring upon **you** [Ahaz], and upon **your people**, and upon **your father's house**, days that have not come, from the day that Ephraim departed from Judah; even the king of Assyria." (Isaiah 7:17).

Then Why The Blessing?

Then why the blessing? According to this interpretation, it is because of God's immutable promise before to his servant David, as David said, "And now, LORD, you are God, and have promised this goodness to your servant: And now it has pleased you to bless the house of your servant, that it may be before you forever: for you have blessed, LORD, and **it shall be blessed** forever." (1 Chronicles 17:26-27). And God not only promised good to the house of David, but he also promised good to Israel in the same place, "For your people Israel you have made your own people **forever**; and you, LORD, have become their God." (1 Chronicles 17:22).

But this blessing, is it to all the sons of Jacob, or even all the house of David, in every generation? It cannot be, without denying what was quoted before from the Scriptures, as well as the plain history of Israel. But this blessing is ultimately, and forever, to bless a **remnant** of Israel. The Lord spoke of this remnant and the Messiah in Isaiah 65:9-11: "And I will bring forth a seed out of Jacob, and out of Judah one to inherit my mountains: and my chosen shall inherit it, and my servants shall dwell there. ... my people that have sought me. But you are they that forsake the LORD".

According to the name of Isaiah's son, Shearjashub, it is *the remnant* that shall return. For God spoke of the one who is acceptable to him, saying, "but to *this* man will I look, even to him that is poor and of a contrite spirit, and trembles at my word." (Isaiah 66:2). Nevertheless, God's good and eternal promise to bless the house of David, and Israel, does affect his dealings with all the sons of Jacob in every generation. God said this just prior to the previously quoted verses in Isaiah 65:8, "Thus saith the LORD, 'As the new wine is found in the **cluster**, and one says, Destroy it not; for a blessing is in it: so will I do for my servants' sakes, that I may not destroy the whole.'"

A Future Blessing

According to this interpretation, the blessing refers to some future good that God will do because of his good and eternal promise to the house of David and Israel, despite their evil deeds. The purpose of the sign is that the house of David might believe in a greater deliverance, which he will work out in spite of them, when from David's seed he raises up a Savior for Israel. He will do it even though Solomon and his sons did not keep God's commandments and statutes, and as a result Solomon's kingdom could not be established, and the house he built must be cast out of God's sight. He will deliver them for his own sake and for his servant David's sake (e.g., Isaiah 37:35). He will do it even as he says when speaking about performing that good thing he had promised to David, "Not for your sakes do I this, saith the Lord GOD, be it known unto you: be ashamed and confounded for your own ways, O house of Israel." (Ezekiel 36:32).

But Why Promised Here?

But why would God promise to give this sign in the middle of Isaiah 7, where the setting is Ahaz' self-righteous rebellion against God, and the ensuing trouble brought on Judah?

Actually, Isaiah contains many prophecies of the Messiah, which are commonly given in this kind of setting. It is as if God repeatedly underscores his statement in Ezekiel, "Not for your sakes do I this, saith the Lord GOD, be it known unto you: be ashamed and confounded for your own ways, O house of Israel." (Ezekiel 36:32). It is the same thing shown by the record of Solomon and his sons. If Israel will dwell safely and move no more, it will not be brought to pass by them – but in spite of them. Neither David nor his son Solomon will build a house for the Lord to dwell forever – but God will build David a house.

A Different Interpretation Of The Sign

This theme of the book of Isaiah begins in the first chapter. In the midst of talking about the sins of the seed of Jacob, and the trouble and destruction God will bring on them as a result, the Lord spoke of the days of the promised Messiah. "Ah sinful nation, a people laden with iniquity, a seed of evildoers, children that are corrupters: they have forsaken the LORD, they have provoked the Holy One of Israel unto anger, they are gone away backward. ... Your new moons and your appointed feasts my soul hates: they are a trouble unto me; I am weary to bear them. ... Your princes are rebellious, and companions of thieves: every one loves gifts [bribes], and follows after rewards: they judge not the fatherless, neither does the cause of the widow come unto them. Therefore saith the Lord, the LORD of hosts, the mighty One of Israel, Ah, I will ease me of mine adversaries, and avenge me of mine enemies: And I will turn my hand upon you, ... and they that forsake the LORD shall be consumed. ... And it shall come to pass in the last days, that the mountain of the LORD'S house shall be established in the top of the mountains, and shall be exalted above the hills; and all nations shall flow unto it." (Isaiah 1:4,14,23-25,28, 2:2)

The Lord spoke here to the house of David, and the sign is certainly given to them. But the Hebrew Scriptures record the promise of this sign for those in every generation who seek the God revealed in them.

Who Is The Almah?

But some may object, "It says, 'ha'almah', meaning '*the almah*'. The definite article 'ha' implies '*the almah*' is present. But Mary, of course, was not present when the Lord spoke those words to the house of David through Isaiah." However, that is not a valid objection. In Hebrew, "ha" could also be used to refer to "a certain" almah – a definite, but as yet unknown, almah. Note also that the Lord did not find it important to mention anyone being present except Isaiah, his son Shearjashub, and Ahaz. For example, he did not say to Isaiah in verse 7:3, "Go forth now to meet Ahaz, you, and Shearjashub your son, and your wife," nor, "Go forth now to meet Ahaz and his wife."

Is She, Or Is She Not, A Virgin?

But is "ha'almah" a virgin? Some may object, "Even though 'almah' (עלמה) **can** refer to a young woman who is a virgin, it does not **have to** refer to a virgin. If God wanted to make this sign clear, why didn't he use 'b'tulah' (בתולה), the Hebrew word found in other places in the Hebrew Scriptures (including Isaiah) which unambiguously refers to a virgin?" As mentioned before, there is disagreement about the common meaning of "almah" at the time the prophet spoke about 2700 years ago. It is interesting to know that it cannot be proved that the Scriptures *ever* use almah to refer to other than a young, virgin woman. This same statement cannot be made about b'tulah – for in some places (e.g., Isaiah 37:22) it metaphorically refers to a nation. If b'tulah had been used in Isaiah 7:14, this would **not** make it unambiguously refer to a virgin woman, but rather a different objection could be raised, "This refers to a child which will come out of the virgin 'daughter of Zion,' referred to later in Isaiah 37:22. It refers to a *nation* – not a literal virgin *woman*."

But consider the assumption at the heart of this objection, "If God wanted to make this sign clear, ...". It is not necessarily true that God wanted to make this sign clear.

A Different Interpretation Of The Sign

Why Is This Sign So Hard To Understand?

God has written *many* things hard to understand in the Hebrew Scriptures. It is not necessarily expected that God wanted to make this sign easy to understand. But who does God say will understand those things necessary to know him; that is, who does God say will find him? "you shall find him, if you seek him with all your heart and with all your soul." (Deuteronomy 4:29). This passage, as many like it, describes those who will find God as those seeking with an earnest effort. Those who occasionally take a passing glance, and like to trust in those who have an appearance of knowledge, or have opinions desirable for some other reason, should know this: they themselves will **not** know the God of Abraham, Isaac, and Jacob.

The Lord sent the prophet Jeremiah to "Stand in the gate of the LORD'S house, and proclaim there this word, and say, Hear the word of the LORD, … Trust not in lying words, saying, 'The temple of the LORD, The temple of the LORD, The temple of the LORD, are these.' … Behold, you trust in lying words, that cannot profit. Will you steal, murder, and commit adultery, and swear falsely, and burn incense unto Baal, and walk after other gods whom you know not; And come and stand before me in this house, which is called by my name, and say, 'We are delivered to do all these abominations?' Is this house, which is called by my name, become a den of robbers in your eyes? Behold, even I have seen it, saith the LORD. But go now unto my place which was in Shiloh [the first place of the tent of meeting, or tabernacle of the congregation], where I set my name at the first, and see what I did to it for the wickedness of my people Israel." (Jeremiah 7:2,4,8-12). These individuals, to whom God sent the prophet Jeremiah, were walking in sin. However, because they could go and stand in the house that Solomon built for the name of the Lord, where the ark of the covenant rested, they trusted that God was pleased with them personally. But God in his mercy sent Jeremiah to warn them.

However, the Lord told Jeremiah about a terrible problem, "you shall speak all these words unto them; but **they will not listen to you**" (Jeremiah 7:27). Because of this problem, the Lord commanded Isaiah, "Now go, write it before them on a tablet, and note it in a book, that it may be for the latter day for ever and ever: That this is a rebellious people, lying children, children that will not hear the law of the LORD: Which say to the seers, 'See not'; and to the prophets, 'Prophesy not unto us right things, speak unto us smooth things, prophesy deceits: Get you out of the way, turn aside out of the path, cause the Holy One of Israel to cease from before us.'" (Isaiah 30:8-11).

When God sent Isaiah to Judah, as written in the Isaiah 6:8-10 passage which precedes Isaiah 7, he told him, "Make the heart of this people fat, and make their ears heavy, and shut their eyes; **lest** they see with their eyes, and hear with their ears, and understand with their heart, and convert, and be healed." It is not surprising then, to find the sign promised in the immediately following chapter hard to understand – which those with heavy ears would not be able to hear. Jesus quoted this passage from Isaiah 6 when his disciples asked him why **he** spoke in ways hard to understand. He also explained, "**For** ... with the ears they **heard** heavily, and their eyes they **closed, lest** they see with the eyes, and hear with the ears, and understand with the heart, and be converted,

A Different Interpretation Of The Sign

and I heal them" (Matthew 13:15). Jesus spoke such that those not **willing** to hear, will **not** hear.

Ahaz was not willing to believe; therefore, God did not give a sign to help him believe. This sign, which is hard to understand, is given only to those willing to seek in order that they might find. It is given only to those willing to believe.

When Was This Sign Supposed To Take Place?

As previously mentioned, finding the blessing of this sign promised in the midst of a passage of reproof and describing hard consequences leads one to expect the blessing is for a later time. Without question, the sign will take place in the days when there is one born who is called "With Us God." However, there is no indication in the Hebrew Scriptures that this happened before they were completed. This did happen in the days of Jesus' birth, for that is one of his names (as Matthew 1:23 says, and as we hear him called today, "Immanuel"). Jesus has more than one name, even as the Messiah is given more than one name in the Hebrew Scriptures.

In the New Testament Scriptures (written in Greek), the Greek name for Jesus is the same as the Greek name for Joshua (compare Matthew 1:21 with Hebrews 4:8). It is also the same as the Greek name used for Joshua by the Jewish scholars who translated the Pentateuch into Greek in the Septuagint many years prior to Jesus' birth (compare Matthew 1:21 with Numbers 13:16 in the Septuagint). Therefore, Jesus' Hebrew name is "Joshua" (יהושע). It is interesting to consider that Joshua brought Israel into the Promised Land,

The Mysterious Sign to the House of David

which Moses could not do because of his sin (Numbers 20:12, Deuteronomy 32:48-52). It is also interesting to know that Joshua's given name was actually Hoshea, but Moses called him Joshua: "Moses called Hoshea [הושע] the son of Nun, Joshua [יהושע/Jesus]." (Numbers 13:8,16).

But It Says: Ha'almah *With* Child

But some may object, "It says, 'behold, ha'almah **with child** and shall bear a son'. The Hebrew word הרה, meaning "with child", is properly translated as being a present condition, meaning she is already pregnant, and cannot refer to something which would happen 700 years later when Mary was pregnant with Jesus." The Jewish translators of the ArtScroll Tanach and JPS 1917 felt this could refer to a future event, because they translated it "will become pregnant" and "shall conceive". And הרה certainly has the appearance of being used to refer to a future pregnancy when it is used in Judges 13:3ff.[4] Actually, there is disagreement over the part of speech and form of the Hebrew word "הרה". Regardless, the following two sections will show that the English translation "ha'almah with child" does *not* require ha'almah to be with child at the time the prophet spoke.

---

[4] If you are interested in looking at that passage, take particular note of what is said in verse 3. Also, consider that the reason the woman is told about her (impending?) conception is because there are certain things she must in no way eat during her pregnancy (verses 4, 7, and 14). It does not appear to make sense to tell her about these dietary restrictions after she has already been pregnant for a time.

Prophecies In The Past Tense

It is not necessary for the text to be translated in the future tense in order to refer to a future event. For the Lord God speaks of things that have not yet occurred as if they already are, and brings them to pass. He said to Abraham, "for the father of many nations I **have made** you." (Genesis 17:5). In Deuteronomy, he spoke of the future disobedience of the sons of Israel as if it had already occurred. For example, the Lord described to Moses what the sons of Israel would do after he brings them into the land he was giving them, "For when I shall have brought them into the land which I swore unto their fathers, that flows with milk and honey; and they shall have eaten and filled themselves, and waxen fat; then will they turn [future] unto other gods, and serve them, and provoke me, and break my covenant." (Deuteronomy 31:20). But then he spoke as if it had already happened, "Do you thus requite the LORD, O foolish people and unwise? is not he your father that has bought you? has he not made you, and established you? ... He made him ride on the high places of the earth, that he might eat the increase of the fields; and he made him to suck honey out of the rock ... But Jeshurun waxed fat, and kicked: you are waxen fat, you are grown thick, you are covered with fatness; then he forsook God which made him, and lightly esteemed the Rock of his salvation. They provoked him to jealousy with strange gods, with abominations provoked they him to anger. ... And when the LORD saw it, he abhorred them ... And he said, I will hide my face from them ... They have moved me to jealousy with that which is not God; they have provoked me to anger with their vanities: and I will move them to jealousy with those which are not a people; I will provoke them to anger with a foolish nation." (Deuteronomy 32:6,13,15-16,19-21).

The Mysterious Sign to the House of David

The LORD is the one who *named the king*, Cyrus, who would command Jerusalem and the temple to be rebuilt, before that man was *ever born*, or Jerusalem even destroyed: "That saith of Cyrus, He is my shepherd, and shall perform all my pleasure: even saying to Jerusalem, 'You shall be built'; and to the temple, 'Your foundation shall be laid'. Thus saith the LORD to his anointed, to Cyrus, … '… **that you may know** that I, the LORD, which **call you by your name**, am the God of Israel. For Jacob my servant's sake, and Israel my chosen, I have **even called you by your name**: I have surnamed you, though you have not known me. I am the LORD, and there is none else, there is no God beside me: I girded you, though you have not known me: **That they may know** from the rising of the sun, and from the west, that there is none beside me. I am the LORD, and there is none else.'" (Isaiah 44:28-45:1,3-6).

As an important side note, the fulfillment of this prophecy about Cyrus then is a tremendous sign – given to us all by God – for the purpose of helping us to believe that Isaiah did indeed write the words of the Lord, as he said, and as Hezekiah believed, but Ahaz refused to believe. Search and see. After this prophecy was written, the Chaldeans needed to conquer Judah (the beginning of the Babylonian captivity), and destroy Jerusalem and the temple. Persia needed to take control of the Chaldeans' kingdom, and a child named Cyrus needed to be born, and ascend to the throne of Persia. That king Cyrus was the one who gave the decree to rebuild Jerusalem and the temple – according to the word of the Lord by the mouth of his prophet Isaiah.

The Sign: Ha'almah With Child

Matthew 1:18-22 says that the following happened in order to fulfill the sign promised in Isaiah 7:14: the Holy Spirit begot a child in Mary, a virgin, and the angel of the Lord revealed that she would bear a son who would be the Savior of his people. This statement in Matthew 1:22 is made prior to the record of the child's birth, or any mention that one of his names would be "With Us God." Then according to this interpretation, the tremendous sign that the Lord says he will give is contained in the first five words, "[Therefore, shall give the Lord himself to you a sign;] behold, the virgin with child". Behold the tremendous sign that the Lord himself will give: a virgin who is with child. The words that follow the sign – "and will bear a son …" – supply additional information.

Who Is The Holy Spirit?

The Holy Spirit who begot the child Jesus in Mary, according to Matthew 1:18,20 and Luke 1:34-35, is God's Spirit, and not "another god." For when David said, "The **Spirit of the LORD** spoke by me, and **his word** was in my tongue." (2 Samuel 23:2), he also made it plain that it was, "**The God of Israel** [who] said …" (2 Samuel 23:3).

Or have you not heard that God, "whose name is Holy" (Isaiah 57:15), has a Spirit? This is the Spirit about which David pleaded with God saying, "Cast me not away from your presence; and take not your Holy Spirit from me." (Psalm 51:13(11)). When Israel inquired 'where is our God?', in Isaiah 63:11, they asked, "where is **he** that put **his** Holy Spirit within him?" Elihu said, "The Spirit of God has made me, and the breath of the Almighty has given me life." (Job 33:4). And it was the Spirit of the LORD who brought Ezekiel to the valley of *very* dry bones, and who caused flesh to cover those bones, and gave them life (Ezekiel 37:1-14, though some translations render the Hebrew word רוח "breath" in places there where "Spirit" is what is meant by that word – as it is in verse 1). And, according to the New Testament Scriptures, the Spirit of God begat a living son in the womb of a virgin.

Are There Any Other Passages Which Speak Of A Virgin With Child?

This interpretation, if true, explains another mysterious passage, found in the midst of a chapter in Jeremiah which speaks throughout of the days of the Messiah, "turn again, O virgin of Israel, turn again to these your cities. **How long will you go about, O backsliding daughter? for** the LORD has created a new thing in the earth, A woman shall compass [תסובב] a man." (Jeremiah 31:21-22). The Hebrew verb translated "compass" in the above passage is used in 147 verses in the Scriptures, and generally means "to go around." Whatever it refers to when used here, it is a wonder, it is "a new thing in the earth," it is something that has not occurred before. In its context, it is something that should have caught the attention of the backsliding daughter Israel, but she is slow to recognize ("How long ..."). A son springing up inside a virgin, the virgin having had no physical contact with the world which could cause that to happen, is a new thing in the earth: a woman, alone, encompassing a man.

A Different Interpretation Of The Sign

Whose Son Would This Be?

If ha'almah who is with child, and is the subject of this tremendous sign that is given by God, is indeed a virgin, then the son whom she carries has not been begotten by any man. And, if God gives this sign, then it seems readily to follow that this son – who has not been begotten by any man – has been begotten by God. This is what the New Testament asserts.

If that is true, then it could indicate a deeper meaning behind what the Lord told David concerning the Messiah (who is of David's seed), "I will raise up your seed after you" (1 Chronicles 17:11). The Hebrew words used to describe God raising up (קום) David's seed (זרע) here, are the same words used to describe Onan raising up seed to his brother (who had died): "And Judah said unto Onan, 'Go in unto your brother's wife, and marry her, and raise up seed to your brother.'" (Genesis 38:8). In Onan's case, he was told to raise up seed to his brother by begetting a child which would be counted, or deemed, his brother's seed. The words used in 1 Chronicles 17:11, "I will raise up your seed after you", could indicate that God would raise up seed to David in that he himself would beget a child which would be deemed David's seed. (Whether a seed begotten by God could be deemed David's seed according to the Hebrew Scriptures will be addressed later.) There is only one other place in the Scriptures where those particular words are used to describe one raising up (קום) another's seed (זרע). That is where God spoke of raising up Solomon in 2 Samuel 7:12. However, it was made clear in that place that the seed would be from David's own body, "I will set up your seed after you, which shall proceed out of your body" (2 Samuel 7:12).

Chapter Five

The Name Of This Son

There is a very unusual feature of the name of this son, "With Us God", in most copies of the Hebrew text. No other man's name in the Hebrew Scriptures has this feature except the Messiah's. Two Hebrew names of God – אל (transliterated El, usually translated God) and יהוה (transliterated YHWH, usually translated LORD) – are so special that no man in the Scriptures, except the Messiah, has either of those names appear separately and unmodified in his own name. Many men have a word for their name that *contains* those words (for example, "Joel" – "יואל"), or contains a form of them. However, no other man has either one of those words, *separate* and *unmodified*, as a word in his name.

The Use Of אל And יהוה In Names

These two words (אל and יהוה) appear more than 5500 times in the Scriptures. They are so special that the Hebrew

Scriptures use them *very* sparingly in the names of any other things (again, speaking of their use separately and unmodified).

There are only two physical places having one of those words in its name. The mount of the LORD, in Genesis 22:14, is named "The LORD Will See [יהוה יראה]". And in Genesis 28:19, Jacob named the place where God appeared to him Bethel, which being translated is, "The House Of God [בית-אל]". Some translations have Jacob *renaming* that "place: 'God [אל] The House Of God'" in Genesis 35:7. But it seems very surprising to call a place "God …". For it is written, "I am God [אל] and there is **none else**." (Isaiah 45:22). Also, eight verses later, Genesis 35:15 repeats "Jacob called the name of the place where God spoke with him, Bethel." However, there are other possible translations of the Hebrew in Genesis 35:7, "ויקרא למקום אל בית-אל", which do not rename the place "God …". One such rendering is "and he called the place of God, Bethel". But the prefix "ל" in "למקום" can also be translated "toward". Therefore, another possible rendering is, "[And he built there an altar,] and he called toward the place of God, Bethel: [because there God appeared unto him]" (Genesis 35:7). This seems more likely, since the *purpose* of building the altar was to call on God. And the practice of calling toward the house "where God is" is mentioned by Solomon in 1 Kings 8:29. There Solomon asks God to "listen to the prayer which your servant shall make toward this place".

There is only one city that will have one of those words in its name. The city described at the end of Ezekiel, where the Lord "will dwell in the midst of the sons of Israel forever"

(Ezekiel 43:7), is named "The LORD Is There [יהוה שמה]" (Ezekiel 48:35).

There is only one altar with such a name. The first altar Moses built, he named, "The LORD Is My Banner [יהוה נסי]" (Exodus 17:15). Some translations have two other altars with such names: "God, The God Of Israel" (Genesis 33:20) and "The LORD Of Peace" (Judges 6:24). Again, it seems very surprising to call an altar "God" or "The LORD". However, the Hebrew in each passage, "ויקרא-לו", which is rendered in those translations "and he called it", could also be rendered "and he called to [with a third person singular masculine suffix]". Therefore, it seems more likely that the intended meaning of "ויקרא-לו אל אלהי ישראל", is "[And he erected there an altar,] and he called to God, the God of Israel", rather than, "[And he erected there an altar,] and he called it God, the God of Israel."

In the Hebrew Scriptures, the word אל sometimes *refers to*, but is never the name of, a false "god" (e.g., "a foreign god", Psalm 81:10(9)). This occurs about eight times, although the exact number depends on interpretation. That use accurately describes what some men have made it to themselves – their god. But in truth it "is not God" (Deuteronomy 32:21). "For who is God [אל] except the LORD [יהוה]?" (2 Samuel 22:32).

However, the Messiah has one of those words (אל or יהוה) in at least two or three of his names given in the Hebrew Scriptures. There is no other living being with this distinction in the Scriptures. Further, at least one or two of the Messiah's names are **the same as** a name of **God**. This is so significant, that it is worth taking some care to examine where the Hebrew Scriptures give these names of the Messiah.

A Name Of The Messiah In Jeremiah

Jeremiah 23:5-6 gives one of the Messiah's names when it speaks of days to come after the Babylonian captivity: "Behold, the days come, saith the LORD, that I will raise unto David a righteous Branch, and a King shall reign and prosper, and he shall execute judgment and righteousness in the earth. In his days Judah shall be saved, and Israel shall dwell safely: and this is his name whereby he shall be called, 'The LORD Our Righteousness [יהוה צדקנו].'" (Jeremiah 23:5-6). Recall that the first temple, the house that Solomon built for the name of the Lord, was destroyed during the first years of the Babylonian captivity, and afterward, not one of Solomon's sons have reigned as king.

This name for the Messiah is repeated in Jeremiah 33:16. However, some translations of that verse make it seem like it is a name for Jerusalem. But the context of the verse, together with the Hebrew words themselves, indicate it is another reference to the Messiah's name previously given in Jeremiah 23:6. Verses 15 and 17 there certainly speak of that same righteous Branch, the Messiah, "In those days, and at that time, will I cause the Branch of righteousness to grow up unto David; and he shall execute judgment and righteousness in the earth." (Jeremiah 33:15). And in verse 16 his name is repeated: "In those days shall Judah be saved, and Jerusalem shall dwell safely; and this is he who will call to her: 'The LORD Our Righteousness' [אשר-יקרא-לה יהוה צדקנו]

וזה]." This verse declares the name of the one who will call her to salvation and safety.

A Name Of The Messiah In Isaiah 9

Another of the Messiah's names is given in Isaiah 9:5(6). "For a child has been born to us, a son given to us: and the government is upon his shoulder: and his name is called Wonderful, Counselor, **Mighty God** [אל גבור], Everlasting Father, Prince of Peace. Of the increase of his government and peace there shall be no end, upon the throne of David, and upon his kingdom, to establish it, and to support it with judgment and with justice from henceforth even forever." (Isaiah 9:5-6(6-7)).

A number of English "translations" of this verse have corrupted the plain name given to this man by the Hebrew Scriptures. For there is no dispute about what is written in Hebrew: "ויקרא שמו פלא יועץ אל גבור אביעד שר-שלום". Perhaps some translators feared to call the name of a man "**Mighty God**," not understanding how it could be right for a man to have that name. However, if a translator changes the words in a passage of the Scriptures which he does not understand, into words that make sense to him but are incorrect, how will those who read the changed words learn what the passage means?

Differing English Translations

But what about those who seek to understand a passage in the Hebrew Scriptures, yet find their understanding depends on which of two different English translations is correct? It is easy to obtain copies of the untranslated Hebrew text. But what about those who don't speak Hebrew? There are a number of tools to help someone whose native language is English determine which translation more faithfully represents what God spoke through his prophet. An English "Interlinear Bible" (e.g., ISBN 1-878442-82-1) offers an English translation of each Hebrew word beneath each of the words in the Hebrew Scriptures. (If you get one, remember that, unlike English, Hebrew is written from right to left.) Besides providing a "third opinion," it can point to the specific Hebrew word(s) which need(s) to be studied in order to determine which translation is correct. An "Analytical Hebrew Lexicon" (e.g., ISBN 0-913573-03-5) not only gives English definitions of Hebrew words, but also shows the root word for each form of Hebrew word in the Scriptures, and describes the inflection of each form.

Our children learn our native language by listening to us talk. Then, we can learn how God speaks by listening to him. How did God use a given Hebrew word in the Scriptures? A "Hebrew Concordance" (e.g., ISBN 1-565632-08-7) shows every verse in the Hebrew Scriptures where a given Hebrew word is used, and may further group those verses according to similar inflection of the root word. Today, these references can be searched for and ordered over the Internet from on-line booksellers such as Barnes & Noble or Amazon.

The Messiah: Mighty God

The one spoken of in this passage, with such a great name as **Mighty God**, must be the Messiah; for it is said that there is "**no end**" to "the increase of his government and peace" "upon the throne of David", "to establish it … from **henceforth even forever**." This is the second name for the Messiah that has one of those two special words in it, separate and unmodified: Mighty God [אל גבור]. Further, this two-word name is also **a name for God**, found in the very next chapter: Isaiah 10:21. It is interesting to consider some of the Messiah's other names given in Isaiah 9:5(6), for example: Everlasting Father

Hezekiah: Not Mighty God

There are some who say this passage refers to Hezekiah, because the language "a child has been born" is past tense. But the words "Of the increase of his government and peace there shall be **no end**," give the strong impression that this cannot refer to the unremarkable length of Hezekiah's reign – which was stained by sin and paying tribute to the king of Assyria. Because of Hezekiah's sin, God told Hezekiah that the days would come when all he had would be taken to Babylon, and some of his sons would be eunuchs serving the king of Babylon (2 Chronicles 32:24-26,31, 2 Kings 20:14-20 – a sin after the manner of that described in Ezekiel 23:40-41). Sometimes the expression "no end" in the Hebrew Scriptures is not used to refer to something that literally never ends, but is used metaphorically for something that seems to go on and on and on. But Hezekiah's reign as king, twenty-nine years, was not abnormally long for a king's reign.

His son Manasseh, who reigned after him, and who "seduced them [Judah] to do more evil than did the nations whom the LORD destroyed before the sons of Israel" (2 Kings 21:9), reigned almost twice as long – "fifty-five years" (2 Kings 21:1). Further, in the *middle* of Hezekiah's reign, "in the fourteenth year of king Hezekiah did Sennacherib king of Assyria come up against all the fenced cities of Judah, **and took them**" (2 Kings 18:13), and the king of Assyria laid tribute on Hezekiah, and "At that time did Hezekiah cut off the doors of the temple of the LORD" (2 Kings 18:16).

Further, the increase and peace of Mighty God's kingdom is "to **establish** it … from henceforth even **forever**." This confirms that Hezekiah cannot be Mighty God. But this *was* what God promised of the Messiah's kingdom to David, as quoted earlier, "and his throne shall be **established forever**" (1 Chronicles 17:14, where the words in bold are translated from the same Hebrew words in the two passages). Hezekiah's kingdom (which is Solomon's) was **not** established forever – neither could it be. The reason for this is because Solomon was not "constant to do my commandments and my judgments, as at this day." (1 Chronicles 28:7). Rather, because of Hezekiah's own sin God told him all he had would be taken to Babylon.

The Past Tense

Then why the past tense in this prophecy in Isaiah 9:5(6), as if the child had already been born and the government was on this one's shoulder? As said before, prophecies of things yet to come are sometimes spoken in the past tense in the Hebrew Scriptures. A careful look at this prophecy's context confirms that it is indeed speaking of a future event in the past tense. At the beginning of Isaiah 8, Isaiah prophesies during the days in which the government is on Ahaz' shoulder. He prophesies of the future trouble God will bring on the head of Syria (Damascus) and the head of Ephraim (Samaria) by the king of Assyria. By means of the king of Assyria, God will deliver Judah from the two kings as he had promised in Isaiah 7 (see Isaiah 7:7-9 and Isaiah 8:4, and a description of its fulfillment in 2 Kings 16:7-9). However, because of Ahaz' rebellion against God, he also prophesies of the severe trial he will bring on Judah, also by means of the king of Assyria (see Isaiah 7:17ff and Isaiah 8:6-8, with an indication of its fulfillment in 2 Chronicles 28:19-21 and 29:8-9). Similarly, in Isaiah 8:21-22 a coming hardship is prophesied in the future tense ("... And they shall look unto the earth; and behold trouble and darkness ..."). But then notice that a *subsequent* glory is also prophesied, beginning in Isaiah 8:23(9:1), and a transition is made to speaking as if it is already accomplished ("The people that walked in darkness have seen a great light" Isaiah 9:1(2)).

The Name in Isaiah 7:14

This feature of some of the Messiah's names (containing either אל or יהוה as a separate and unmodified word) may also be found in the name given to the son in Isaiah 7:14, "With Us God." The copies of the Hebrew Scriptures we have differ in whether the name in Isaiah 7:14 is written as two separate words or one word: "עמנו אל" or "עמנואל". An example of a Hebrew text having it as two separate words is the Biblia Hebraica Stuttgartensia, endorsed by the Jewish Publication Society.⁵ If the name is indeed written as two separate words, then, in accordance with this interpretation of the sign, it is a third name of the Messiah having one of those two special words in it – אל.

But if he is not the Messiah, then **who is** this man who is given such a great name; a man about whom the Scriptures say nothing else except perhaps in Isaiah 8:8? For in the passage in Isaiah 8:8, where Isaiah prophesies of the severe trial to be brought on Ahaz and all Judah by means of the king of Assyria, the name is mentioned only one more time. "Now therefore, behold, the Lord brings up upon them the waters of the river, strong and many, even the king of Assyria, and all his glory: and he shall come up over all his channels, and go over all his banks: And he shall pass through Judah; he shall overflow and go over, he shall reach even to the neck; and the stretching out of his wings shall fill the breadth of **your land**, 'With Us God'." (Isaiah 8:7-8). It is natural to think the one named "With Us God" in Isaiah 8:8 is this same man. But when it is observed that the passage calls the land of Judah **his** land (and it does so at a time when Ahaz is king), it raises the possibility that it is **God** who is called by the same name here. It raises the possibility that it is a name for both the Messiah and God – who will eventually deliver Judah from even this trial, "for God is with us" (Isaiah 8:10 – the last time those two words are ever found together in the Hebrew Scriptures).

---

⁵ Although the Hebrew name in Isaiah 7:14 is transliterated in the Greek New Testament where the verse is quoted (Matthew 1:23), the New Testament Scriptures were originally written without anydivisionsbetweenwords. Therefore, the New Testament is silent on this aspect of the name. However, it immediately follows the transliterated name with the words, "which is, being interpreted, 'With Us God'", implying that the meaning of this child's name is not incidental, but has particular significance.

Why Would He Be Called "With Us God"?

If the Holy Spirit of God begot this son, so that God is his literal father, then it follows that he is, in essence, not merely a man, but also God. This last line of reasoning was why "the Jews sought the more to kill him, because he [Jesus] ... said ... that God was his father, [thereby] making himself equal with God." (John 5:18). This reasoning does not imply that God became anything *less* than the Almighty and everywhere-present God when he begot the man Jesus. But it does mean that he *additionally* took on the likeness of a man, in all becoming similar to us (apart from sin). God appeared in the form of a man in times past (e.g., Ezekiel 1:25-2:4). But this is something more than just appearance, it is the one who made the world, becoming flesh and coming into the world (these things are explicitly said in the New Testament in Philippians 2:6-8, Hebrews 2:14-18, 4:15, and John 1:1-14).

That would explain why this child would be called "With Us God." And it may also explain how the words literally translated in Isaiah 7:14, "shall give the Lord himself to you a sign", could be read not only as an underscoring that the Lord himself would *give* the sign, but that he (himself) is the sign. In other words, the sign given by God, a child in a virgin, begotten by God, would be the Lord – himself.

Consider what a tremendous sign this is! It was a tremendous sign previously offered to Ahaz – unique in all the Hebrew Scriptures in its circumstances, and exceptional in the encouragement to Ahaz to ask a sign however great he desired. Now that Ahaz has refused, and God speaks of a sign he will give, should we expect it to be anything less than Ahaz may have ever asked? Could it have ever even entered Ahaz' *thoughts* to ask for such a tremendous sign as this one?

Chapter Six

Could God Become A Man?

Could God become a man? The true question is not whether God could change himself into being *just* a man. The question is: could the God of the Hebrew Scriptures, without changing or setting aside in any way his other attributes, *also* become a flesh-and-blood man? It is not a question of *ability* on God's part, but rather *possibility*: is it possible for God to become a man, given what he has said in the Hebrew Scriptures he will and will not do?

For example, in some sense God has the *ability* to say anything. However, one of the things he *has said* is, "God is not a man that he should lie; neither the son of man, that he should repent: has he said, and shall he not do it? or has he spoken, and shall he not make it good?" (Numbers 23:19). God makes a comparison here between himself and all men, that is, all "the sons of man [אדם/Adam]" (Proverbs 8:4). God has said that he has never, nor will ever, repent or lie, like every man does, but will do according to what he has said.

Therefore, in another sense, it is *not possible* for "the righteous God" (Psalm 7:10(9)) to lie.

Therefore, God could not become a man who would lie, like every other man, nor sin like every man ("for there is no man which does not sin" 2 Chronicles 6:36). If he *were to* become a man, then it would have to be true of that man that "he had done no sin, and deceit was not in his mouth" (Isaiah 53:9) – as it is said of the "man" (Isaiah 53:3) spoken of in Isaiah 53. But this statement about the man spoken of in Isaiah 53 raises a question. If every "son of man" lies and sins, then who is this man prophesied about? God also calls the man spoken of in Isaiah 53:11 "my righteous servant". There is no one else in the Hebrew Scriptures whom God calls, "my righteous servant". God says, "my servant David" in many places (e.g., 2 Samuel 7:8), but never "my righteous servant David."

It is unexpected to read in the very next verse that this righteous man was "numbered with transgressors" (Isaiah 53:12). Though in truth he was **not** a transgressor, he was numbered with them. The reason for this is also given in that verse (for convenience, some verb inflections are shown in brackets here), "he caused his soul to be poured out [Hiphil preterite] unto death: and he was numbered [Niphal preterite] with transgressors; and he lifted up [Kal preterite] the sin of many, and for transgressors to cause him to make **intercession** [Hiphil future]" (Isaiah 53:12). This reason is also explained in previous verses there, "But he was wounded for our transgressions, he was bruised for our iniquities: … for he was cut off out of the land of the living: **for the transgression of my people was he stricken**." (Isaiah 53:5,8). As said before, the past tense of this passage does not require that this had already happened at the time the prophet spoke. And in verse 11 it says, "he **shall bear** their iniquities", showing that this action was not completed at the time Isaiah spoke. The time at which this would come to pass is said to be, "**when** you [the LORD] shall make his soul a **guilt-offering** [אִם־תָּשִׂים אָשָׁם נַפְשׁוֹ]" (Isaiah 53:10). The Hebrew word here for guilt-offering is the same word used, for example, in Leviticus 14:25: "And he shall kill the lamb of the guilt-offering". But this righteous man who poured out his soul unto death, who was cut off out of the land of the living, how is it that he subsequently could make intercession for transgressors (future tense), and how could he receive the many blessings which God also speaks here of giving him *because of* his work (including prolonged days and seed, verse 10)? And if God's righteous servant is the Messiah, how is it then that the promise made to David about this one could be fulfilled, "And I will make him stand in my house and in my kingdom forever" (1 Chronicles 17:14), if he was put to death? But others ask, how could a man having a mortal body stand in God's house and reign in God's kingdom forever? This is not the place to write of that mystery, but more will be said about it later.

But God Does Not Change

We know then, that the Lord will do what he has purposed and promised; he does not lie, nor does he change his mind. This attribute of God is also spoken of in 1 Samuel 15:29, and Malachi 3:6. Some say that Malachi 3:6 shows that God could never become a man: "For I am the LORD, **I change not**; therefore you sons of Jacob are not consumed. Even from the days of your fathers you are gone away from my ordinances, and have not kept them." (Malachi 3:6-7).

The three words "I change not" give that impression. But this passage in Malachi observes that the sons of Jacob are not consumed. The reason why one would expect them to have been consumed is because "from the days of your fathers you are gone away from my ordinances, and have not kept them." God gives a reason here for why they *have not* been consumed ("therefore ..."). Is the reason they have not been consumed because God would never become a man? No, but it is because the Lord will bring about what he has purposed and promised despite all the provocation of the sons of Israel that he do otherwise. That is what this means, "I change not; therefore you sons of Jacob are not consumed." Just as the Lord spoke through Jeremiah, "Behold, the days come, says the LORD, that **I will perform** that good thing which **I have promised** to the house of Israel and to the house of Judah." (Jeremiah 33:14). Immediately following this affirmation in Jeremiah, the Lord speaks of how he will raise up the Messiah, "In those days, and at that time, will I cause the Branch of righteousness to grow up unto David" (Jeremiah 33:15).

A summary of this is that there is no changing with God, like the changing with every man. Although he punishes Israel in the heat of his anger for their sins at one season, then has pity on them and redeems them for the sake of his servant David and because he has set his love on them – God is not fickle. In all things he acts according to his good and unchanging character, and in faithfulness to what he has said he will do. It is in this sense the Hebrew word for "change" [שנה] is used in Malachi 3:6: "I change not". That same Hebrew word for "change" is used in a similar way in the description of how David *did change* his behavior to pretend himself insane before the king of Gath (1 Samuel 21:14(13), Psalm 34:1).

But You Shall Make No Image Of God

Some say that the warning to Israel in Deuteronomy 4:15-16 shows that God would never take on a human form: "Take you therefore good heed unto yourselves; for you saw **no form** on the day that the LORD spoke unto you in Horeb out of the midst of the fire: Lest you corrupt yourselves, and make you a graven image, **the form of any figure**, the likeness of male or female". There are two separate, though related, issues here. Does this statement mean God would **never** manifest himself to people with a form? And if God did manifest himself, for example, in a human form, would that mean he had broken his own commandment, "You shall not make a graven image" (Deuteronomy 5:8)?

Although God did not manifest himself to all Israel on that day with a form, he manifested himself to Moses with a form at other times, "Hear now my words: If there be a prophet among you, I the LORD will make myself known to him in a vision, and will speak unto him in a dream. My servant Moses is **not so** ... With **him** I speak mouth to mouth, by an appearance, and not in riddles; and the **form** of the LORD he beholds" (Numbers 12:6-8). The Hebrew root word for the form of the Lord which Moses looked upon (ותמנה), is the same as that of the form that Israel saw not (תמונה). But why is this surprising? For God also manifested himself to Isaiah with a form, "In the year that king Uzziah died I saw also the Lord sitting upon a throne, high and lifted up, and his train filled the temple. ... Then said I, 'Woe is me! for I am undone; because I am a man of unclean lips, and I dwell in the midst of a people of unclean lips: for mine eyes have seen the King, the LORD of hosts.'" (Isaiah 6:1,5). Ezekiel 1:25-2:4 is an example where God appeared in the form of a man.

Does that mean God has transgressed his own command, that we should not make a graven image? The command forbids us from making an image intended to represent God. But if God manifests himself in a form, it is not a form made by human hands, and then said by those who formed it, "This is your god," as Aaron, Moses' brother and the first high priest, did in Exodus 32:4. Jesus is not a "graven" image, an image fashioned by human hands. John, a Jewish man who was with Jesus continually for several years, said of him, "and we beheld his glory, the glory as of the only begotten of the Father, full of grace and truth." (John 1:14). Of the Messiah it is written in the Psalms, "You are fairer than the sons of men: grace is poured into your lips" (Psalm 45:3(2)). No other man is described with such terms in the Scriptures (e.g., grace poured into his lips).

Is It Possible The Messiah Could Be God With Us?

Some have said that the Hebrew Scriptures prove it impossible for God to become a man – but in fact they do not. Rather, a number of passages indicate the Messiah, a man, would be God with us. A few of them have been discussed previously. Here are a few more.

In Psalm 110, "A Psalm of David" (Psalm 110:1), David speaks of the Messiah. David in the Spirit calls the Messiah his Lord, saying, "The LORD said unto my Lord, 'Sit at my right hand, until I make your enemies your footstool.'" (Psalm 110:1). No man in the Hebrew Scriptures has called a son he has begotten "my Lord". When David calls the Messiah here "my Lord," he says he is a servant of this one called his son. But if the Messiah is only David's son, and not also God with us, then why does the patriarch David, to whom the promises were made, make himself his son's servant?

See also what great things the same psalm says about the Messiah three verses later, "The LORD has sworn, and will not repent, you are a ***priest* forever** after the order of Melchizedek." (Psalm 110:4). A comparison is made here of the Messiah to Melchizedek (whose name means "King of Righteousness"). Melchizedek, who was not a Levite, was both a king and priest of the most high God before the Law was given: "And Melchizedek, king of Salem [where God's abode is: Psalm 76:3(2)] ... he was the priest of the most high God." (Genesis 14:18). To Melchizedek, even the patriarch Abraham, "gave him tithes of all." (Genesis 14:20). Now the priests who serve(d) on the earth according to the Law must be from the tribe of Levi, and they do not serve forever because of their deaths. But the Messiah is from the tribe of Judah. He serves as priest only after, "he caused his soul to be poured out unto death: ... and he lifted up the sin of many, and for transgressors to cause him to make intercession [future]" (Isaiah 53:12). Isaiah 53 says that he makes intercession after his death. After "he was cut off out of the land of the living" (Isaiah 53:8), God raised him up on the third day, and he ascended into the heavens – where he sits at the right hand of the LORD, as a king and priest forever.

Some say that Psalm 110, written by David, refers to David himself. They say he wrote it for others to sing about him – their lord. But David had not ascended into the heavens to sit at the right hand of the LORD. And David was never a priest, much less a priest forever.

And see what things the Lord speaks of the Messiah through the prophet Micah, "But you, Bethlehem Ephratah, though you are little among the thousands of Judah, yet out of you shall he come forth unto me that is to be ruler in Israel; whose goings forth have been **from of old [מקדם], from the days of forever**." (Micah 5:1(2)). This statement is true of no other man. It is written, "Are you not from of old [מקדם], LORD my God, my Holy One?" (Habakkuk 1:12, as also Deuteronomy 33:27, Psalm 55:20(19), and Psalm 74:12). It is interesting to note something said in Micah about conditions during the (first) days of the Messiah's reign, "for now shall he be great unto **the ends of the earth**. ... And the remnant of Jacob shall be **among the nations**, in the **midst** of many people" (Micah 5:3,7(4,8)).

But You Shall Have No Other Gods

There is a serious warning written in the Law, "You shall walk after the LORD your God ... If your brother, the son of your mother, or your son, or your daughter, or the wife of your bosom, or your friend, which is as your own soul, entice you secretly, saying, Let us go and serve other gods, which you have not known, you, nor your fathers ... You shall not consent to him" (Deuteronomy 13:5,7,9(4,6,8)). Some say that a Jewish person who believes Jesus is the promised Messiah – "With Us God" – is doing this very thing. However, the Jewish Messiah is not said to be "With Us Another God," but the son of the God of Abraham, Isaac, and Jacob – "With Us The LORD God."

Abraham knew God, and he was called the friend of God (2 Chronicles 20:7). Search your heart and ask yourself, do you truly know the God whom Abraham, Isaac, and Jacob knew? This question is not whether you know some things about God, but whether you know **him**. Are you his friend?

In the Hebrew Scriptures, the fathers of Israel are said to be: "your fathers, Abraham, Isaac, and Jacob" (Deuteronomy 1:8). Not *all* Jewish fathers have known God. For the Lord said through Joshua, "put away the gods which your fathers served" (Joshua 24:14). In fact, it was the whole congregation of the sons of Israel that took up stones to kill Joshua (whose Greek name is Jesus) and Caleb, when those two alone pleaded with them not to rebel against the Lord by refusing to enter the Promised Land (Numbers 14:6-10). As a result, God swore that not one of those men would enter into the land he had sworn to their fathers (Numbers 14:22-24, 32:11-14). According to his oath, Joshua and Caleb were the only men brought up out of Egypt, from 20 years old and over, who later entered the land: "But among these there was **not a man of them** whom Moses and Aaron the priest numbered, when they numbered the sons of Israel in the wilderness of Sinai. For the LORD had said of them, 'They shall surely die in the wilderness.' And there was not left a man of them, **save** Caleb the son of Jephunneh, and Joshua the son of Nun." (Numbers 26:64-65). If Jesus is the promised Jewish Messiah, the Savior of Israel, woe to those who reject him.

Chapter Seven

Who Can See A Virgin With Child?

But there is another, very important, objection to the interpretation that the tremendous sign is "behold, the virgin with child". Some may say, "That would be a tremendous sign, for a virgin to be with child. But how could the house of David see that sign?"

Did The House Of David See Mary?

When Mary was pregnant with Jesus, "it came to pass in those days, that there went out a decree from Caesar Augustus, that all the world should be registered ... And Joseph also went up from Galilee, out of the city of Nazareth, into Judea, unto the city of David, which is called Bethlehem, because he was of the house and lineage of David, to be registered with Mary his betrothed wife, being with child" (Luke 2:1,4-5). Joseph lived in Nazareth, but he and Mary, his betrothed wife, had to be registered in Bethlehem since they were of the house of David. Neither they nor many of the house of

The Mysterious Sign to the House of David

David lived in that city, so when they arrived, "there was no room for them in the inn." (Luke 2:7). When "Mary ... being with child" entered Bethlehem, she saw all the house of David, called out from among all the tribes and houses of Israel, assembled in this one place. And the house of David beheld her.

A special assembly of the house of David like this is not recorded any other time in the Scriptures. Perhaps, by chance, someone read aloud from the book of Isaiah in the synagogue on the sabbath, "Hear now, O house of David ... shall give the Lord himself to you a sign; behold, ha'almah with child, and will bear a son" (Isaiah 7:13-14). God had gathered them all together, and placed the sign in their midst.

How Could The House Of David Know The Sign Was Fulfilled?

But some may still object, "How could the house of David know that the Lord had brought the sign to pass?" The answer raises an important aspect of this sign, consistent with the context of the passage and the character of God. This is a tremendous sign – but it is a sign only to those desiring to seek the truth, to those willing to believe. For those wanting to close their eyes could dismiss it out of hand, saying, "It can't be proved that it happened." Only those willing to believe would do the honest work of searching it out, examining the witnesses to it, in order that they might believe. At the time the Lord parted the Red Sea, that was a sign that the God of Abraham, Isaac, and Jacob is God – to those both willing and unwilling to believe (e.g., Exodus 14:11-13,18,30-31). But now, the parting of that Sea is a sign that the God of Israel is God only to those willing to believe. For there are witnesses that it did, in fact, happen. But those witnesses must be sought out by a heart that seeks the Lord; a heart willing to believe.

What Is The Evidence?

There is quite a bit of evidence that Jesus was born of a virgin. Although this is not the place to write at length of the evidence, for the benefit of those desiring to consider it, various kinds of evidence are mentioned here.

There are two broad categories of witnesses: those providing evidence that Mary was a virgin, and those providing evidence of other things which, if true, would show that Mary did not conceive by a man. This second category includes evidence that God begot Jesus, or that Jesus is God with us. For if God begot Jesus, then Mary did not conceive by a man. Similarly, if Jesus is God with us, then a man could not have begotten him. This second category also includes evidence that Jesus is the Messiah, taken together with evidence that the Messiah would be born of a virgin, or begotten by God, or would be God with us.

The house of David at that time had a special witness that God had fulfilled this sign. Perhaps, since the house of David was all gathered in Bethlehem, someone spoke in the synagogue on the sabbath about Bethlehem's unique significance, reading from the prophet Micah how the Messiah would be born there, "But you, Bethlehem Ephratah, though you are little among the thousands of Judah, yet out of you shall he come forth unto me that is to be ruler in Israel; whose goings forth have been from of old, from the days of forever."

(Micah 5:1(2)). According to the prophecy, while Joseph and Mary were in Bethlehem to be registered, Mary gave birth to Jesus: "And so it was, that, while they were there, the days were accomplished that she should be delivered. And she brought forth her firstborn son [Jesus]" (Luke 2:6-7). On the day Jesus was born, "the angel of the Lord" appeared to shepherds watching their flocks at night, "and the glory of the Lord shone round about them" (Luke 2:9). The angel told them, "behold, I bring you good tidings of great joy, which shall be to all people. For unto you is born this day in the city of David a Savior, which is Christ the Lord." (Luke 2:10-11). [Note: In the New Testament, "Christ" is the English translation of the Greek word for Messiah, as explained in John 1:41.] The angel gave the shepherds a sign by which they could recognize this newborn son, and they went to Bethlehem and found it as the angel had said. "And when they had seen it, they made known abroad the saying which was told them concerning this child. And all they that heard it wondered at those things which were told them by the shepherds. ... And the shepherds returned" (Luke 2:17-18,20). And so it was "made known abroad" by these shepherds – what the angel of the Lord spoke concerning the Messiah, the Lord, who had been born in Bethlehem that day. This was a special witness to the house of David in those days. There were other witnesses to people at that time, such as the prophecy of the priest, Zacharias (Luke 1:67-75), and the words of the prophetess Anna (Luke 2:36-38).

Among the evidence available to us today, are the same witnesses to many other signs the Lord gave. There is the testimony of men – the prophets and the apostles – whose words may be read in the Hebrew Scriptures or New Testament today by those desiring to discern whether they were deceivers, or holy men of God who spoke the words of God. The Lord says this concerning his word spoken by the prophets, "Hear, for I will speak of excellent things, and from the opening of my lips, right things. For my mouth shall speak truth; and wickedness is hateful to my lips. All the words of my mouth are in righteousness; there is nothing twisted or perverse in them." (Proverbs 8:6-8).

The Hebrew Scriptures confirm that a man would be born of a virgin (this passage in Isaiah 7:14, together with Jeremiah 31:22). The second psalm also says that God would beget the Messiah, "I will declare the decree: the LORD said to me, 'You are my son, this day have I begotten you. Ask of me, and I shall give ... the ends of the earth for your possession.'" (Psalm 2:7-8). In this psalm, the prophet who wrote the psalm told of something the Messiah, who had not yet been born, would say in a day which had not yet occurred. Some may say the prophet did not speak of the Messiah here, but of Israel. But in this psalm it is a *man* who speaks through the prophet, "I will declare the decree: the LORD said to me ...". Some may say the prophet speaks of a man like Solomon here, for God said of Solomon, "I shall be to him for a father" (2 Samuel 7:14). But God did not say to this man here, "I shall be to you for a father," but he says here that there is *one day* in which God *begat* him. This man is the Messiah, and no other, for he is a man to whom God says he will give "the ends of the earth for your possession."

Jesus' words recorded in the New Testament are evidence, as well as all the miracles and signs he did confirming them. Some officers who were sent by the Pharisees and chief priests to seize Jesus, returned empty handed, saying, "Never did a man so speak as this man." (John 7:46). For Jesus did not speak as other prophets, who spoke the words of God at specific times, but *every* word Jesus spoke was the word of God (John 3:34, 12:48-50, 14:10, 7:16-18, 8:45-47). If he was God with us, it could not be otherwise. The first four books of the New Testament record what Jesus said and did in the days of his flesh. It is *never* recorded that he said, like other prophets, "Thus says the Lord, …", but instead, "I say to you …".

His empty tomb is a testimony. "He is not here: for he is risen, as he said. Come, see the place where the Lord lay", testified the angel (Matthew 28:6). And there is the eyewitness testimony of those Jewish men who ate and drank with him after he was raised from the dead. They did not receive riches or glory from the world for their testimony, but received insults and persecutions in this life – as have all the prophets. Many were put to death saying this same thing, even to death, that they, "ate and drank with him after his rising again out of the dead. And he commanded us to proclaim to the people and to solemnly witness, that it is he who has been marked out by God judge of the living and the dead. To this one all the prophets witness, to receive remission of sins through his name, everyone believing in him." (Acts 10:41-43).

A Bible is easily obtained by anyone interested in searching out these things. For example, you can order a hardcover New King James Version (one of the most literal of the popular modern translations), from www.bn.com (Barnes & Noble online, ISBN 0-8407-0055-5) for only about $6. Alternatively, if someone gave this book to you, that person would probably also gladly obtain a Bible for you. Read any or all of the first four books in the New Testament (each of which is only about 20 - 30 pages in length). If you seek the Lord, then you can pray to him, asking him to show you the truth.

Chapter Eight

Curds And Honey

In the two verses following Isaiah 7:14 it is written, "Curds and honey he shall eat that he may know to refuse the evil and choose the good. For, before the lad shall know to refuse the evil and choose the good, the land will be forsaken that you hate before both her kings." (Isaiah 7:15-16). This passage states that "he" will eat curds and honey. For this diet to be mentioned here in the Scriptures, it must be significant. This is a peculiar diet of curds and honey, it is not that at one time he had curds, and another time honey, as could be said about many people.

What is the reason given for eating curds and honey? The unexpected reason given is, "*that he may know* [לדעתו] to refuse the evil and choose the good." Why would eating those foods help someone to know that he should refuse what is evil and choose what is good? Yet, the words immediately following confirm this reason, "**For**, *before* the lad shall know to refuse the evil and choose the good ...". It is said here that there is a period of time that this lad does not know he should choose what is good and refuse that which is evil. The state of this lad before eating curds and honey sounds similar to the problem God earlier charged against the "inhabitants of Jerusalem, and men of Judah", "that call evil good, and good evil" (Isaiah 5:3,20).

When Shall He Eat Curds And Honey?

The lad will certainly eat curds and honey after the two kings leave. Further, it is implied that it is *only* after they leave that he will eat this peculiar diet. For eating them should teach him to refuse the evil and choose the good – yet he will not have learned that before the two kings leave.

Who Shall Eat Curds And Honey?

Since these two verses follow verse 14, it is expected that the "he" referred to is the son to be born. However, it is surprising to think Jesus would need to eat something "that he may know to refuse the evil and choose the good." Further, since there is a period of time *before* this lad knows to refuse evil, that implies a time he could *choose* evil. But Peter, another Jewish man who was with Jesus continually for several years before he was crucified, said of him, "who did no sin, neither was guile found in his mouth" (1 Peter 2:22). This, of course, is different from all other men – who are "the sons of man [אדם/Adam]" (Proverbs 8:4), whose father is the sinful, and "dead", Adam (Genesis 2:17). For even David himself says, "I was brought forth in iniquity, and in sin did my mother conceive me" (Psalm 51:7(5)). But of the Messiah, the Hebrew Scriptures say, "I was cast on you from the womb: you are my God from my mother's belly." (Psalm 22:11(10)), and "From the womb the Lord called me, from my mother's belly he mentioned my name." (Isaiah 49:1). In order to understand the basis for another, more likely "lad", it is necessary to look first at what is spoken to Ahaz in the remainder of this chapter, in verse 17 and following.

The Severe Trial

In Isaiah 7:17 and following, the Lord told Ahaz of a severe trial he would bring on him, his people, and the house of David after the two kings depart, by the hand of the king of Assyria. "The LORD shall bring upon **you** [singular], and upon **your people**, and upon **your father's house**, days that have not come, from the day that Ephraim departed from Judah; even the king of Assyria." (Isaiah 7:17). As mentioned previously, the trial is a result of Ahaz refusing the good, and choosing the evil. The Lord would deliver them from the two kings of their present trial, as he promised. But since Ahaz, and Judah with him, are determined to continue in their evil ways, he will also bring a subsequent trial on them. What do you think? If you have a child who does evil, and you do good to him only, yet he does not stop, and then you do not also bring consequences on him for his evil doings, how will he ever learn to stop doing the evil, and rather choose the good? In this case, Ahaz was beyond hope; but there was hope that a remnant in Judah and the house of David would repent of their ways in the future.

The rest of Isaiah 7 describes the destruction and waste the king of Assyria will bring upon Judah. For example, "And it will be in that day, it will be every place where there is

The Mysterious Sign to the House of David

[currently] a thousand vines worth a thousand silver, it shall be for the briars and the thorns. ... all the land shall be briars and thorns. And all the hills which were hoed with the hoe, you shall not come there for fear of briars and thorns" (Isaiah 7:23-25). If the crops are all destroyed, what will the people eat during this time of severe oppression from the king of Assyria? The answer is given in verses 21 - 22, "And it will be in that day, a man will keep alive a heifer of the herd and two sheep. And it will be, from the plenty of making milk, he shall eat curds; for **curds and honey he shall eat, everyone who is left in the land**." (For the cows and sheep will be able to eat in those fields, according to Isaiah 7:25.) Now, the "he" who shall eat curds and honey in Isaiah 7:22, is "everyone who is left in the land" of Judah.

Ahaz' name is not explicitly mentioned in Isaiah 7 after he refused God's gracious command. As observed previously, this is also the last time he is personally spoken to in the book of Isaiah. It is somewhat confusing in this last part of Isaiah 7 that "you" changes from meaning the house of David, to meaning Ahaz, without mentioning Ahaz' name to mark the change. Although there is a particular reason for Ahaz' name not to be mentioned here, there are other places in the Scriptures where there is an "unmarked change" in who "you" is. For example, when the Lord spoke in Isaiah 37:22b-29, "you" meant the king of Assyria. But in the immediately following Isaiah 37:30-35, "you" suddenly meant Hezekiah, and "he" meant the king of Assyria. There is no interruption in the flow or indication of this change in who "you" is, other than the substance of what was said. In Isaiah 7, there is no question that Ahaz is spoken to in verse 17, and that the house of David is spoken to in verses 13 and 14. The question then arises: when did the Lord begin speaking to

Ahaz again? The answer is made clear by looking at the Hebrew text, for when the Lord spoke to the house of David in verses 13 and 14, he addressed them as a plural "you" (four times). Ahaz, of course, is addressed as a singular "you" in the Hebrew text. Therefore, Ahaz was the one addressed in verse 16 by the singular "you". And verse 16 is a continuation of what was spoken in verse 15, for it starts, "For …". Therefore, verse 15 also must have been spoken to Ahaz. Then, the house of David was spoken to only in verses 13 and 14, and the rest was spoken to Ahaz. "Curds and honey he shall eat that he may know to refuse the evil and choose the good. **For,** before the lad shall know to refuse the evil and choose the good, the land will be forsaken that **you** [Ahaz, singular] hate before both her kings. The LORD shall bring upon **you** [Ahaz, singular], and upon **your people** [Judah], and upon **your father's house** [the house of David], days that have not come, from the day that Ephraim departed from Judah; even the king of Assyria." (Isaiah 7:15-17).

He Shall Eat Curds And Honey

When it is understood that verses 15 and 16 were spoken to *Ahaz* about this future *trial*, whereas the sign of verse 14 was spoken rather to the *house of David* about a future *blessing*, it is then *not expected* that verses 15 and 16 would refer to the son in the sign of the blessing. Then, who is "he"?

In the Isaiah 37 passage referenced previously, where "you" changes from meaning the king of Assyria to meaning Hezekiah, "he" is used after the change to refer to the previous "you" – the king of Assyria. It seems likely that is the case here also – that "he" in verse 15 similarly refers to the previous "you": the house of David. In Hebrew, a house is masculine in gender and is referred to as "he" (e.g., "טמא הוא בבית", "[it is a fretting leprosy] in the house: unclean is he", from Leviticus 14:44).

The Hebrew words translated "Curds and honey he shall eat" in Isaiah 7:15, are *identical* to the Hebrew words "curds and honey he shall eat" seven verses later in Isaiah 7:22. The "he" who shall eat curds and honey in Isaiah 7:22, is "everyone who is left in the land" – all the house of David and Judah who survive. These two passages refer to the same future trial brought on them by the king of Assyria, after the two kings causing their present trial have departed. A reason for this affliction is given in verses 15 and 16 – this "diet of affliction" will teach the survivors to rather "refuse the evil and choose the good". As described earlier, this did happen during Hezekiah's reign.

But is it reasonable to think then, that the house of David could be referred to as a "lad [נער]" in verse 16? It is, because Israel is referred to as "a lad" in Hosea 11:1, "When Israel was a lad [נער], then I loved him". The Hebrew word translated "lad" here is different from the words translated "child" and "son" in verse 14.

Chapter Nine

A Man's House

The concept of the house of a man is found throughout the Scriptures. For example, there is the house of Abraham, the house of Israel, the house of Aaron, and the house of Jonathan. Joshua declared that he and his house would serve the Lord (Joshua 24:15). It is written, "Behold, the days come, saith the LORD, that I will make a new covenant with the house of Israel, and with the house of Judah: Not according to the covenant that I made with their fathers in the day that I took them by the hand to bring them out of the land of Egypt; which covenant of mine they broke" (Jeremiah 31:31-32). Because of many significant passages like this one, it is important to spend some time to understand what the house of a man is in the Scriptures.

Previously, the house of David was described in a word to consist of those born in David's house, women married to men in the house of David, and their slaves (not hired servants). Here will be given a more complete answer and explanation of what a man's house is according to the Hebrew Scriptures.

The House Of David, The Seed Of David, The Sons Of David

One way the Scriptures show the definition of a man's house is by using that term in passages where they also give a description of the individuals it denotes. Before looking at some of the passages showing the definition, it is helpful to know that in the Hebrew Scriptures the terms "house (בית) of a man" and "seed (זרע) of a man" are almost always synonymous. However, in the Scriptures, the seed of a man is generally **not** synonymous with those begotten by the man (his biological children). As will be shown, the seed of a man (or house of a man) does not necessarily encompass all those whom the man has begotten. Furthermore, the seed of a man may encompass individuals whom the man has *not* begotten.

Some passages use the terms "house of a man" and "seed of a man" interchangeably to denote the same individuals. For example, God commanded Abraham that he should circumcise all the males of his seed, "This is my covenant, which you shall keep, between me and you and **your seed** after you; Every male among you shall be circumcised." (Genesis 17:10). The ones Abraham circumcised, which were the males of his seed, were, "every male among the men of the **house of Abraham**" (Genesis 17:23). As for, "the uncircumcised male whose flesh of his foreskin is not circumcised, that soul shall be cut off from **his people**; he has broken my covenant." (Genesis 17:14). Then, as used here, the house of Abraham means the same thing as the seed of Abraham. The house of a man is used synonymously with the seed of a man in Ezra 2:59 (as also Nehemiah 7:61), "but they could not show their father's house, and their seed [that is – same thing – whose seed they were], whether they were of Israel".

The equivalence of a man's house and a man's seed is also seen in the special instruction given to priests. Only those of the house of Aaron could eat of the heave offering of the holy things (when they were clean), "I have given them to you, and to your sons and to your daughters with you, by a statute forever: every one that is clean in **your house** shall eat of it." (Numbers 18:11). Those same people are also referred to as Aaron's seed eight verses later, "All the heave offerings of the holy things … have I given you, and your sons and your daughters with you, by a statute forever … to you and to **your seed** with you." (Numbers 18:19). Notice that they are also called, "your sons and your daughters". Those of a man's house, or seed, may also be called his "sons" or "daughters" in the Hebrew Scriptures. Although all the males of a man's house are called his "sons" in the Hebrew Scriptures, the term "son" is also used other ways not described here.

Who Are They?

But who are those counted the house of a man, the seed of a man? That is defined in the passages describing who should be circumcised, and who could eat of the heave offering of the holy things. For those passages use both the terms "house" and "seed", and also describe specifically who is encompassed by those commands, so that they can be properly carried out. To summarize the definition, it is those who are "born in the house", or purchased by a man in the house (that man's slave, not his hired servant). A woman is of the house of her husband, and so only a man's unmarried daughters, or his widowed or divorced daughters who had no children and who have returned to his house, are deemed his seed. Accordingly, we read, "And all the men of his house, **born in the house**, and **bought with money of the stranger**, were circumcised with him." (Genesis 17:27). And, "But if the priest buy any soul with his money, he shall eat of it, and he that is born in his house: they shall eat of his bread. If the priest's daughter also be married unto a stranger, she may not eat of an offering of the holy things. But if the priest's daughter be a widow, or divorced, and have no child, and is returned unto her father's house, as in her youth, she shall eat of her father's bread: but there shall no stranger eat thereof." (Leviticus 22:11-13). A difference is described between a slave (who is of the house) and a hired servant (who is not of the house), and between one who is born in the house (who is of the house), and one who lives in the house only (who is not of the house): "There shall no stranger eat of the holy thing: [that is] one who dwells with the priest, or an hired servant, shall not eat of the holy thing." (Leviticus 22:10).

Born In The House

The term "born in the house" does not refer to the *physical place* a person is born; it refers to whether a child is born *of a woman* who is *of the house*. Therefore, "those born in the house" and "those begotten by a man of the house" may denote different individuals. A child is the seed of the man in whose house it is born, even if a different man begot the child (although with one exception to be explained shortly). Because of this definition, it is not an issue in determining a child's house and lineage, whether or not the child was indeed *begotten* by the man in whose house the child was born. Perhaps this is because a man and his wife have "become one flesh" (Genesis 2:24). Whatever the reason(s), this is a mercy to a sinful and adulterous generation, where also false accusations and suspicion would abound. The exception: there is a way a man may beget a child of his wife, who subsequently, in a sense, is born of his wife in his house, and yet that child is deemed the seed of another man, and of that other man's house. If a man marries his dead brother's childless wife, their first child is counted his brother's seed (see for example Genesis 38:8-9, which was formalized in the Law in Deuteronomy 25:5-9).

A Slave

Today, the concept of a slave is foreign to most people, so it may be worthwhile to point out that a slave (unlike a hired servant) is a possession by definition. Today we usually think of possessions as "things," but in this case it is not a thing, but a person who is owned. A person who is owned by a master is, in that way, someone who is a *member* of the master's house. Therefore, Abraham called Eliezer, "the son of my house [בֶּן־בֵּיתִי]" (Genesis 15:3). Consider what a position Abraham's slaves had – that they are counted sons of Abraham. Yet they had a master they must obey. But yet again – unlike many masters – Abraham's slaves had a good, wise, kind, just, and wealthy master. We might understand if one of his slaves had been offered freedom but refused, saying, "Where shall I go? Yes, I must labor here, and keep your commands, but I would need to labor wherever I go. The work you give me to do is profitable because of your wise direction of it, and your abundant resources. Because I labor here for you, I do not need to worry about whether I will have enough to eat. It is well with me here in your house, you provide for all my needs and those of my family. I am safe with you. Moreover, you teach me God's ways, and lead me in paths of righteousness. Freedom is good, but being a member of Abraham's house is better." It is recorded in the Scriptures that one of Abraham's slaves pleaded with God *privately*, "LORD God of my master Abraham, I pray you … show kindness unto my master Abraham." (Genesis 24:12).

An Example

The definition of a man's house is displayed in the book of Joshua, in the place where the harlot Rahab asked the two men of Israel, "Now therefore, I pray you, swear unto me by the LORD, since I have shown you kindness, that you will also show kindness unto **my father's house**" (Joshua 2:12). There are three descriptions given of the members of Rahab's father's house.

Rahab described her father's house saying, "*save alive* my father, and my mother, and my brothers, and my sisters, and all that they have, and deliver *our lives* from death." (Joshua 2:13). Note that "all that they have" means all who belong to them, which includes any born in the house of her father or brothers, or any owned by them (that is, any slaves). It is clear these are *people* being spoken of here – Rahab is not requesting them to deliver the life of a coffee table. Whether or not the house of Rahab's father included slaves, the words recorded here in the Scriptures for our edification ("all that they have") would encompass them if it did.

The two men gave a second description of Rahab's father's house when they confirmed they would keep the oath they had sworn. They described her father's house as, "your father, and your mother, and your brothers, and all the [others of the] house of your father" (Joshua 2:18). Because there was no disagreement between Rahab and the two men of Israel as to *who* was of her father's house, these different descriptions of the members of the house comprise the same people. Rahab's father, mother, and brothers are certainly members of her father's house. Then there are "all the others" of the house of her father, which in this case includes some others "that they have" (whether slaves, or her brothers' seed, or perhaps those born of harlotry in her father's house), as well as her (evidently) unmarried "sisters". There is a good chance that her father's house would have included children born of harlotry, since Rahab was a harlot, and being unmarried was still a member of her father's house (though she apparently did not dwell in his physical house from what is written in Joshua 2:1). It is true that such children would be Rahab's, and those whom "she had." However, since Rahab was of the house of her father, they would also be counted what "her father had;" they would be counted of the seed and house of her father. Therefore, children born of harlotry to Rahab would also be encompassed in the description "all that they [in this case, her father, not her brothers] had".

There is a third description of those of her father's house given, "And Joshua saved Rahab the harlot alive, and the house of her father, and all that she had" (Joshua 6:25). The explicit mention here of those "that she had" gives the impression that there were indeed children of Rahab's harlotry included in her father's house.

Another Example

An understanding of these things explains how it is that when Hosea took a wife who played the harlot, and conceived a son by adultery, the son is called Hosea's: "And the LORD said to Hosea, 'Go, take to you a wife of whoredoms and children of whoredoms: for the land has committed great whoredom, departing from the LORD.' So he went and took Gomer the daughter of Diblaim; which conceived, and bore **to him** a **son**." (Hosea 1:2-3). Hosea's wife was chosen by the Lord to be a picture of Israel. According to this picture, the Lord says of Israel's offspring, "And I will not have mercy upon her children; for they are the children of whoredoms. For their mother has played the harlot: she that conceived them has done shamefully: for she said, I will go after my lovers" (Hosea 2:6-7(4-5)).

But Not All The Seed Of Abraham Is The Seed Of Abraham

Sometimes, the words "seed" or "house" in the Hebrew Scriptures refer only to a special subset of all the seed, or all the house, of a man. Occasionally, though not often, the "seed" of a man refers only to those begotten by a man – his "biological seed". Whenever a seed is described to come from a man's "mayah" (מעה), or "yahrake" (ירך), it means one whom he has begotten (but those words do not have to be present). For example, in the same place where Abraham called Eliezer "the son of my house", he lamented to God, "Behold, to me you have given no seed" (Genesis 15:3). In that place, Abraham spoke of a seed from his own body. But this God assured he would give him, "he that shall come forth out of your own bowels [mayah - מִמֵּעֶיךָ] shall be your heir" (Genesis 15:4).

It is very important to understanding the Scriptures to know another restrictive sense in which "seed" or "house" may be used in them. The "seed of Abraham" is sometimes used to refer only to the seed of the promise, the promised blessing of God to Abraham, "to be God to you and to your seed" (Genesis 17:7). When the Lord told Abraham to heed Sarah's desire to send away Hagar and Ishmael (the son Hagar bore to Abraham), he makes it plain that although Ishmael is Abraham's seed, the seed of the promise would be called through Isaac: "And God said unto Abraham, '... all that Sarah has said to you, listen to her voice; for **in Isaac shall your seed be called**. And also of the son of the slave-woman will I make a nation, because he is your seed.'" (Genesis 21:12-13). There is a use of the term "seed of Abraham" which refers only to those of Abraham's seed who are called by God – those who serve God with the faithful Abraham – all of them, but none other than them. It is Isaac's seed which is deemed the seed of Abraham in this sense. Rebekah also conceived **two** sons from Isaac, Esau and Jacob. But Isaac blessed Jacob, saying, "And God Almighty bless you, and make you fruitful, and multiply you, that you may be an assembly of peoples; and give you the blessing of Abraham, to you, and to **your seed** with you" (Genesis 28:3-4). This was confirmed by the Lord to Jacob: "I am the LORD God of Abraham your father, and the God of Isaac: the land whereon you lie, to you will I give it, and to your seed ... and in you and in your seed shall all the families of the earth be blessed." (Genesis 28:13-14). Then, not all of the seed of Abraham are the seed of Abraham to whom the promise was made, but those whom God shall call.

And Not All Those Of Israel, Are Israel

So also, not all the seed of Jacob (who was also named Israel – Genesis 35:10) are the seed of Israel to whom the promises are made. In other words, when used in the Hebrew Scriptures in this restrictive sense, not all those "of Israel" are "Israel". It is written, "Israel shall be saved in the LORD with an everlasting salvation: you shall not be ashamed nor confounded for all eternity. … In the LORD shall **all the seed of Israel** be justified, and shall glory." (Isaiah 45:17,25). The word seed is used restrictively here to refer to only, but all of, the seed who will be saved. It certainly cannot refer to all the seed of Jacob without restriction, for the first psalm says: "the wicked shall not stand in the judgment, nor sinners in the congregation of the righteous." (Psalm 1:5). But who shall ascend into the hill of the Lord, or stand in his holy place? Is it not those who have clean hands and a pure heart (Psalm 24:3-5)? They are the seed who will receive a blessing from the Lord. When the sons of Israel entered into the covenant which the Lord commanded Moses to make with them, it was written of the man who thinks he will have peace from God, even though he walks in the imagination of his heart: "The LORD will not spare him, but then the anger of the LORD and his jealousy shall smoke against that man, and all the curses that are written in this book shall lie upon him, and the LORD shall blot out his name from under heaven." (Deuteronomy 29:19(20)). Just as "the LORD said unto Moses, 'Whosoever has sinned against me, him will I blot out of my book.'" (Exodus 32:33).

Israel has at times misunderstood this. The Lord complained to Israel through the prophet Malachi about this misunderstanding among them, "You have wearied the LORD with your words. Yet you say, 'Wherein have we wearied him?' When you say, 'Every one that does evil is good in the sight of the LORD, and he delights in them'; or, 'Where is the God of judgment?'" (Malachi 2:17). This misunderstanding is further addressed in Malachi 3:16-20(4:2): "a book of remembrance was written before him for them that feared the LORD ... And they shall be mine, saith the LORD of hosts ... Then shall you return, and **discern** between the righteous and the wicked, between him that serves God and him that does not serve him. For, behold, the day comes, that shall burn as an oven; and all the proud, yea, and all that do wickedly, shall be stubble: and the day that comes shall burn them up, says the LORD of hosts, that it shall leave them neither root nor branch. But unto you that fear my name shall the Sun Of Righteousness arise with healing in his wings".

The Seed Of Falsehood

Corresponding with this restrictive usage of the term "seed of Israel," those of the broader seed of Israel, outside this remnant "seed of Israel," are sometimes called terms such as a seed of evildoers, a seed of falsehood, and the seed of the adulterer: "Ah sinful nation, a people laden with iniquity, a seed of evildoers, children that are corrupters: they have forsaken the Lord" (Isaiah 1:4). "Hear this, O house of Jacob, which are **called by** the name of Israel, and are **come forth** out of the waters of Judah, which swear by the name of the LORD, and make mention of the God of Israel, **but not in truth, nor in righteousness**." (Isaiah 48:1). "Therefore will I number you to the sword, and you shall all bow down to the slaughter: because when I called, you did not answer; when I spoke, you did not hear; but did evil before mine eyes, and did choose that wherein I delighted not. ... And you shall leave your name for a curse unto my chosen: for the Lord GOD shall slay you, and call his servants by another name." (Isaiah 65:12,15). "But draw near hither, you sons of the sorceress, the seed of the adulterer and the whore. Against whom do you sport yourselves? against whom do you make a wide mouth, and draw out the tongue? are you not children of transgression, a seed of falsehood ... but **he that puts his trust in me** shall possess the land, and shall inherit my holy mountain" (Isaiah 57:3-4,13). "Hear the word of the LORD, **you that tremble at his word**; your brothers that hate you, that cast you out for my name's sake, said, 'Let the LORD be glorified': but he shall appear to your joy, and they shall be ashamed." (Isaiah 66:5).

Can Gentiles Be Counted With The Seed Of Israel?

If you are a Gentile, you may be wondering whether you can be counted a seed of Abraham, and an heir of the blessing of Abraham. Yes, you can. This is not the place to write how the Lord brings that to pass. However, it is important to know that those of the Gentiles who serve the God of Abraham are counted a seed of Abraham. Otherwise, how will the promise God spoke to Abraham be fulfilled, "the father of many nations I have made you" (Genesis 17:5)? And not only so, but God also said to Jacob: "your name shall not be called any more Jacob, but Israel shall be your name: and he called his name Israel. And God said unto him, 'I am God Almighty: be fruitful and multiply; a nation [singular] **and** a company [a singular assembly] of nations [plural] shall be of you'" (Genesis 35:10-11).

When God promised to pour his Spirit on the seed of Israel, he made it clear that seed of Israel includes Gentiles who join themselves to the Lord, "I will pour my Spirit upon **your seed**, and my blessing upon your offspring: And **they shall spring up as among the grass, as willows by the water courses. One** shall say, I am the LORD'S; and **another** shall **call himself** by the name of Jacob; and **another** shall subscribe with his hand unto the LORD, and surname himself by the name of Israel." (Isaiah 44:3-5). For the LORD says this, "Assemble yourselves and come; draw near together, you that are escaped of the **nations** ... Look unto me, and be saved, **all the ends of the earth**: for I am God, and there is none else." (Isaiah 45:20,22). And again, "Neither let the son of the stranger, that has joined himself to the LORD, speak, saying, 'The LORD has utterly separated me from his people' ... Even unto them will I give in my house and within my walls a place and a name better than of sons and of daughters: I will give them an everlasting name, that shall not be cut off. Also the sons of the stranger, that join themselves to the LORD, to serve him, and to love the name of the LORD, to be his servants, ... Even them will I bring to my holy mountain, and make them joyful in my house of prayer ... for my house shall be called a house of prayer for all people. The Lord GOD which gathers the outcasts of Israel says, 'Yet will I gather others to him, beside those that are gathered unto him.'" (Isaiah 56:3,5-8).

According to the Hebrew Scriptures, during the days of the Messiah many Gentiles will turn to the Lord. For Isaiah prophesies of a conversation in which the LORD speaks to the Messiah saying, "And now, saith the LORD that formed me from the womb to be his servant, to bring Jacob again to him, Though Israel is **not** gathered [וישראל לא יאסף] ... 'It is a light thing that you should be my servant to raise up the tribes of Jacob, and to restore the preserved of Israel: I will also give you for a light to the Gentiles, that you may be my salvation unto the end of the earth.'" (Isaiah 49:5-6). [Note: Some translators have not translated the Hebrew word לֹא ("not") in their English translation of the above passage from the Hebrew Scriptures. Perhaps they did not understand how that could make sense – that there is a time that the Messiah has come but "Israel is **not** gathered". However, the fact that Israel as a nation is **not** gathered at the time this prophesied conversation takes place, is consistent with the lament of the Messiah in the immediately preceding verse: "Then I said, 'I have laboured in vain, I have spent my strength for nought, and in vain'" (Isaiah 49:4). It is also consistent with the comfort spoken to the Messiah in the previously quoted verse 6.]

Is Jesus The Seed Of David?

God promised David that he would raise up his seed after him to be the Messiah, as quoted earlier, "And it shall come to pass, ... that I will raise up your seed after you, who shall be of your sons; and I will establish his kingdom. ... And I will make **him** stand in my house and in my kingdom **forever**: and his throne shall be established forever." (1 Chronicles 17:11,14). According to this promise, the Messiah must be of the house and seed of David. Is Jesus of the house and seed of David?

Joseph, the betrothed husband of Mary, was "of the house of David" (Luke 1:27). That was why he and Mary were in Bethlehem to be registered at the time of Jesus' birth, as described earlier, "because he was of the house and lineage of

David" (Luke 2:4). Because Jesus was **born in the house of Joseph**, Jesus is "deemed the son of Joseph" (Luke 3:23), and rightly called "the son of Joseph" (John 1:45) – no matter who begot him. Since Joseph is of the house and seed of David, Jesus also is of the house and seed of David. Therefore, Jesus is rightly called "the son of David" (Matthew 1:1).

When the learned Jewish man Saul of Tarsus (who was brought up at the feet of the respected Jewish sage Gamaliel) spoke in the synagogue and said, "Of this man's seed [David] has God according to his promise raised unto Israel a Savior, Jesus" (Acts 13:23), it was not necessary for him to explain how Jesus, whom he **also** declared to them to be begotten by God (Acts 13:33), could be David's seed.

Joseph's House And Lineage

But how is it that Joseph is "of the house and lineage of David" (Luke 2:4)? In Matthew 1:2-16, we read a listing of "who begot whom" from Abraham to David (king of Israel), who begot Solomon, who in turn begot those who reigned as kings over Judah, and on to a man named Matthan, who begot Jacob, who begot Joseph, in whose house Jesus was born. At first glance, this is what one might expect – that the Messiah would be born in the house of the line of kings. But upon closer examination, there are some big problems with this lineage being the Messiah's. To begin with, if the Messiah were one of Solomon's sons, then **Solomon's** kingdom would be established forever. But the promise to establish Solomon's kingdom forever was conditional, "And as for you, **if** you will walk before me, as David your father walked, and do according to all that I have commanded you, and shall observe my statutes and my judgments; **then** will I establish the throne of your kingdom" (2 Chronicles 7:17-18). And God said to Solomon, "you have **not** kept my covenant and my statutes" (1 Kings 11:11). Although God did not take his mercy from Solomon as he did from Saul (2 Samuel 7:15), he could **not** establish Solomon's kingdom forever. Further, Solomon's sons were not left with the entire kingdom – even for the remaining time they were permitted to reign. And eventually the kingdom was completely removed from the house of Solomon with great judgments at the time God cast the house Solomon built out of his sight (2 Kings 25:9). Zedekiah, the last king, is not listed in Matthew, because Nebuchadnezzar slew all of his sons (2 Kings 25:7, Jeremiah 52:10, Jeremiah 39:6). The next-to-last king, Jeconiah (also called Coniah and Jehoiachin), had physical children, and is listed in Matthew 1:11-12, but was "written childless," meaning that none of his seed would ever prosper on the throne of David (Jeremiah 22:30). This is why the Messiah is **never** said to be of the house of Solomon, or to be one of Solomon's sons, in the Hebrew Scriptures.

The mystery is solved by noting that there is a different listing in Luke 3:23-38. There is a list of "whose **son**, or **seed**, was who": "Jesus ... being as deemed the son of Joseph, of Heli, of Matthat, ... of Nathan, of David" (Luke 3:23-24,31). There are some who say this listing in the book of Luke is the lineage of Mary. However, there is no indication of this in the words of the New Testament Scriptures, nor is it relevant in determining Jesus' house and lineage, since Mary was the betrothed wife of Joseph. Although Jacob **begot** Joseph (Matthew 1:16), Joseph is shown here to be "of Heli". Joseph is of the house of Heli, even though Jacob begot him. As described earlier, there are ways that a man may be of the house of a different man from the one who begot him. In Joseph's case, we are not told how that came to be. Joseph's case is similar to Jesus' – who is of the house of Joseph, even though God begot him. Therefore, Joseph (as also Jesus) is "of the house and lineage of David" by way of David's son Nathan (Luke 3:31).

The two different listings in Matthew 1:2-16 and Luke 3:23-38, one of "who begot whom" and one of "whose son, or seed, was who," at first appear to contradict one another. But the apparent contradiction demonstrates something that must be understood if we would also understand how the Messiah is begotten by God, yet is David's seed. This is an example of one of the ways God shows us his word is truth. Unlike men, he purposefully writes to us in mysteries that we do not understand, and things that seem at first to contradict one another. For those who desire to stumble at his word and his ways, he gives ample opportunity. But when he brings what he has decreed to pass, or gives to those who seek him in truth further understanding, we see: "O the depth of the riches both of the wisdom and knowledge of God! how unsearchable are his judgments, and his ways past finding out! For who has known the mind of the Lord? or who has been his counsellor? Or who has first given to him, and it shall be recompensed unto him again? For of him, and through him, and to him, are all things: to whom be glory for ever. Amen." (Romans 11:33-36).

Chapter Ten

What Shall We Say Then?

If you are one seeking the Lord with all your heart, and it seems possible to you that the sign promised in Isaiah 7:14 was fulfilled by Jesus, then you will want to learn more about this man – crucified almost 2000 years ago, but whom many Jews said they saw raised from the dead. Consider that Israel has continued for almost 2000 years with no temple, and no high priest, and no prophets. The Babylonian captivity was a long 70 years, but 2000 years by comparison makes that seem very short. Is it possible that Israel, speaking of the majority, has rejected her Messiah?

Some encourage the Jewish people not to despair, saying that the Lord prophesied of these days in Hosea 3:4, "For many days the sons of Israel will stay with no king, and no ruler, and no sacrifice, and no pillar, and no ephod or teraphim." But this prophecy should not comfort the Jewish people. For it is written in Hosea, "Israel, do not rejoice for joy, like the peoples, for you have gone whoring away from your God" (Hosea 9:1), "for there is no **truth** and no **mercy** and no **knowledge of God** in the land. Swearing and lying and killing and stealing and adultery increase" (Hosea 4:1-2). So the Lord said this, "I will go, let me return to my place until they confess their guilt and seek my face" (Hosea 5:15).

However, no matter what Israel as a nation may do, each man will be judged according to his own ways: "Therefore I will judge you, O house of Israel, each man according to his ways, saith the Lord GOD. Repent, and turn yourselves from all your transgressions; so iniquity shall not be your ruin." (Ezekiel 18:30). A person, whether Jewish or Gentile, does not have to wait for a nation to be right with God, before he himself seeks the Lord. For the LORD says this, "Now, lo, if … a son, that sees all his father's sins which he has done, and considers, and does not do like them: he has not … lifted up his eyes to the idols of the house of Israel, has not defiled his neighbor's wife, neither has oppressed any, … but has given his bread to the hungry, and has covered the naked with a garment, … has executed my judgments, has walked in my statutes; … if the wicked will turn from **all** his sins that he has committed … All his transgressions that he has committed, they shall not be mentioned to him: in his righteousness that he has done he shall live. Have I any **pleasure at all** that the wicked should **die**? saith the Lord GOD: is it not that he should return from his ways, and **live**?" (Ezekiel 18:14-17,21-23).

Perhaps you are thinking at this point, "Yes, that is what I want to do: turn from all my sins and live." It is written of Jesus, "he shall save his people from their sins" (Matthew 1:21). The Messiah is more than a teacher, and more than a prophet. He is a Savior, and he is able to save those who come to him from their sins. It is written, "Neither is there salvation in any other: for there is no other name under heaven given among men [other than Jesus], whereby we must be saved." (Acts 4:12). "For God so loved the world, that he gave his only begotten Son, that whosoever believes in him should not perish, but have everlasting life." (John 3:16).

Jehoshaphat said, "Believe in the LORD your God, so shall you be established" (2 Chronicles 20:20). And he did. But Isaiah warned, "If you will not believe, surely you shall not be established." (Isaiah 7:9).

Then seek the Messiah, the Redeemer of Israel, that you may believe in him. And he will forgive all your sins, and deliver you from them. He will take away your stony heart, and give you a heart of flesh, and put his Spirit within you (Ezekiel 36:26-27, 11:19). He will put his law in your inward parts, and write it on your heart. And he will be your God, and you will truly be among his people (Jeremiah 31:33).

Elisha said, "Say now unto her, '… shall I speak for you to the king, or to the captain of the host?' And she answered, 'I dwell among my own people.'" (2 Kings 4:13)

"Listen, O daughter, and consider, and incline your ear; forget also your own people, and your father's house; So shall the king greatly desire your beauty: for he is your Lord; worship him." (Psalm 45:11-12(10-11))

If you have a friend who may benefit from reading this book, why not give it to him?

You may order multiple copies at a substantial discount by using the order form below. Orders for more than 3 books incur no additional S&H charge.

To order, complete and mail this form to:
Word Of Grace And Truth
P.O. Box 325
Allamuchy, NJ 07820-0325

Orders can be shipped **only** to you, not to a third party.

The Mysterious Sign to the House of David

Your name and U.S. address:
Name_____
Address_____
City_____ State_____ Zip_____

Quantity Ordered: _____
Total Cost of Book(s): _____
(Price is $6.95 per book for less than 3 books,
$3.95 per book for 3 or more books.)

Shipping and Handling: _____
(Enter $2.00 total for S&H for less than 3 books,
and $5.00 for 3 or more books.)

Total: _____

Enclose check made payable to: Word Of Grace And Truth (no credit card or COD orders). New Jersey residents please add 6% sales tax to book cost.

If you have a friend who may benefit from reading this book, why not give it to him?

You may order multiple copies at a substantial discount by using the order form below. Orders for more than 3 books incur no additional S&H charge.

To order, complete and mail this form to:
Word Of Grace And Truth
P.O. Box 325
Allamuchy, NJ 07820-0325

Orders can be shipped **only** to you, not to a third party.

The Mysterious Sign to the House of David

Your name and U.S. address:
Name_____
Address_____
City_____ State_____ Zip_____

Quantity Ordered: _____
Total Cost of Book(s): _____
(Price is $6.95 per book for less than 3 books,
$3.95 per book for 3 or more books.)

Shipping and Handling: _____
(Enter $2.00 total for S&H for less than 3 books,
and $5.00 for 3 or more books.)

Total: _____
Enclose check made payable to: Word Of Grace And Truth (no credit card or COD orders). New Jersey residents please add 6% sales tax to book cost.